Flashback to the Korean War

And God's Promises

MARIE MACALUSO

Carpenter's Son Publishing

Scripture quotations are taken from the Holy Bible, New Living Translation, copyright
©1996, 2004, 2007, by Tyndale House Foundation. Used by permission of Tyndale
House Publishers, Inc., Carol Stream, Illinois 60188. All rights reserved.

Published by Carpenter's Son Publishing, Franklin, Tennessee

Cover and Interior Design by Suzanne Lawing

Printed in the United States of America

978-1-954437-91-3

DEDICATION

This is a testament to our soldiers' courage and humanity
in the face of overwhelming hardships and atrocities! The true
character of the American soldier lies "In God We Trust"!

Isaiah 53:11-12 "And when he sees all that is accomplished by
his anguish, he will be satisfied. And because of his experience …
I will give him the honors of a victorious soldier,
because he exposed himself to death."

Contents

IN EXPLANATION

"You are never right if you do not have a foundation for your testimony in the Word of God" (Smith Wigglesworth). The promises of God in His Word are the testimony of God's presence even in time of war, as experienced and written here.

The memories and the note-taking began after a discussion Sal and I had about nightmares. I told him about my worst nightmare from a time I was about four years old. I had dreamed that I was in bushes on the side of a hill, trying to hide from enemy soldiers walking past me. I always held my breath, and my heart would pound so loud, I was sure the soldiers could hear me.

Upon listening to this, Sal exclaimed, "That's me!"

For my readers to know, the memories came flooding back and I had to be quick to take notes on any paper at hand. His flashbacks would often come unbidden, triggered by hearing a song, a word, or even noises. After a number of years and many shoeboxes full of notes that were like a giant puzzle, I decided to research and write about these experiences and events that were unbelievable.

There was very little information in libraries or bookstores available at that time. I had to start putting notes in chronological order to follow history correctly.

I gradually learned how to refocus Sal's attention by asking key questions. "Who is here with you?" "Is it very cold? Is there snow on the ground?" "Is it raining?" That was the way I had of sorting the events, but more importantly it got Sal grounded again. The more he talked about Korea, it seemed the terrible nightmares lessened, but the flashbacks still came because he was remembering moments that had been repressed and locked deep in his heart. It seemed never ending. At least he didn't have to hide like he did when he was younger by locking himself in his parent's dark basement.

I pored over the *Second Division History Book of Korea*, the 38th Infantry morning reports (roll call of soldiers by company and location), battle reports, *Casualty Book of the Second Division*, articles from the VFW magazines, and even some reports I obtained that, formerly marked "Secret," had been declassified and released upon request from the 38th Infantry Regiment Headquarters. I also contacted the Korean War Association and received letters from many of the men and their families who had served with Sal. Some came to visit us. They confirmed many of the missions that the 38th Infantry was involved in during the war and many remembered Sal.

Among some of the books on Korea was *The Forgotten War* by Clay Blair. It gave me some perspective on what I was writing and offered valuable key facts that supported Sal's experiences. I have also referenced other books and articles that I have read and that helped tremendously.

I hope what I have written has done justice to his memories, and those who fought alongside him. I used nicknames or partial names for privacy reasons. Everything mentioned is true, and it seems more natural to write as though Sal is narrating (my clarifications are in parenthesis).

Luke 1:78-79 – "Because of God's tender mercy, the morning light from heaven is about to break upon us, to give light to those who sit in darkness and in the shadow of death, and to guide us to the path of peace."

INTRODUCTION

If you have a son overseas [in Korea], write to him.
If you have a son in the Second Division, PRAY for him!
~ WALTER WINCHELL, RADIO COMMENTATOR, 1950

The "Land of the Morning Calm" was broken by a heavy rainfall and the crash of mortar shells. The shrieking of metal as hundreds of Russian-built tanks plunged into the defenses along the 38th Parallel was the only warning that North Koreans invaded South Korea, June 25, 1950.

The big tanks crumbled everything in their paths, each firing an 85-millimeter cannon. South Korea's army only had a few 37-millimeter anti-tank guns. With little training and ammunition, the 98,000 soldiers of South Korea were decimated.

By the time the United Nations Security Council began assembling to vote on a cease-fire, the straight road to Seoul, South Korea's capital, lay open to the enemy.

Another calamity was the order to blow up the four bridges over the Han River to protect the south. These bridges were now swarming with a multitude of refugees and military vehicles. The order to cancel this explosion was never received and the demolition was carried through. Uncounted thousands were lost and the last escape route for the battered army of the Republic of Korea (ROKs) was sealed off.

Finally, the cease-fire order was sent out immediately by the U.N.

Our President, Harry Truman, wasn't clear on the American foreign policy regarding Korea. He gave the impression Korea was not part of the United States' area of concern. He gathered his advisors and defense chiefs around him as a result of this conference and ordered General Douglas MacArthur, Commander in Chief of U.S. Forces-Far East, to "take action by Air and Navy to prevent the Inchon-Seoul-Kimpo area from falling into unfriendly hands." American ground troops were not committed because it was hoped that American air and sea forces would be enough to deter the invaders.

By June 28 the tanks and trucks of North Korea clattered into Seoul! The shattered remains of the ROKs now totaled 22,000 men.

The U.N. Council met again on October 7, 1950, authorizing MacArthur to unify Korea and declared that its members furnish assistance as may be necessary to repel the aggression of North Korea. For the first time in history, these members (with the exception of the Soviet Union and Red China) were putting aside their differences to fight together for another nation's right to be free. The first soldiers to do this were Americans. Our forces, badly trained and badly equipped since the end of World War II, were then propelled into assisting, as President Truman's view of the invasion changed and became unacceptable.

The North Korean People's Republic, a Soviet satellite, thought for sure its only opponent would be the dwindling ROK Army.

I personally heard President Truman announce on the car radio, "This is war!" Thinking our involvement would put an end to North Korea's attempts to take over South Korea, he soon started to refer to it as a "conflict." Unfortunately, the North Koreans' aim with the backing of the Soviet Union was to make Korea whole again, under communism. American intelligence had no idea that the Soviets had been building a powerful military force in Asia. Aside from their own men, they were using prisoners of war, or any men gathered up from military takeovers during and after World War II. Such countrymen from Poland, Bulgaria, Hungary, Czechoslovakia, Albania, Romania, and East Germany had no choice but to be used by the communists and North Koreans trained in the USSR.

As always, Americans rose to the challenge. General MacArthur launched his surprise attack with the "Inchon Invasion." This greatly affected and took the wind out of the North Koreans.

General MacArthur's statement, "If we lose the war to communism in Asia, the fate of Europe will be gravely jeopardized," got the attention of the Chinese, who felt their security was seriously menaced! MacArthur meant to push the North Koreans all the way into Manchuria, past the Yalu River, and thus free Korea. Now we had China conferring with Russia! The Chinese would engage us, expecting weapons, supplies, and men from the USSR, though Stalin did not commit the USSR.

Our CIA said the Chinese would not fight. General MacArthur said the same. President Truman thus felt assured. By October 20, 1950, General MacArthur's intelligence declared "indications are that North Korean military and political headquarters may have fled to Manchuria." All thought the war was over.

However, by October 25, 1950, Chinese prisoners were being taken. Intelligence still doubted Chinese involvement. With more and more being taken captive daily, US intelligence and leaders finally became convinced the impossible had occurred. The Chinese were now on the advance.

This was the political arena of the Korean War where my story starts, alongside the Second Indianhead Division, other Americans and Allies engaged in war.

Deuteronomy 33:28 – "So Israel will live in safety, prosperous Jacob in security, in a land of grain and new wine, while the heavens drop down dew."

Tensions in a divided Korea

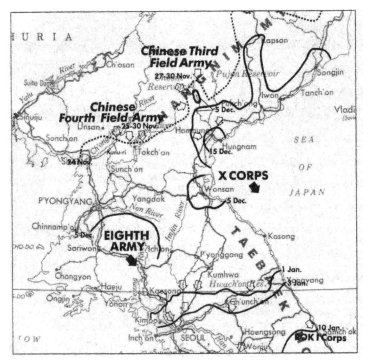

Chinese enter Korea

CHAPTER 1

Choices, Changes, and Chances

He who dwells in the secret place of the Most High
shall abide under the shadow of the Almighty.
~ PSALMS 91:1 (NKJV)

Turning eighteen years' old, my friends and I were experiencing ambitions typical of youth. We wanted to see the world, do something important, and be adventurous. What else was there for teenage boys living in a big city like Brooklyn, New York?

I had already been serving in the U. S. Navy since I was sixteen, spending weekends training at the Brooklyn shipyards. I even traveled to Pensacola, Florida, visiting an uncle who was serving in the Air Force.

Once discharged from the Navy, I intended to reenlist, preferably with another military branch. "Buried at sea" was not for me. All I would take away from the Navy was my comfortable and warm peacoat.

There had to be more to life! Patriotism was at a high since the return of World War II veterans. Four of my uncles served. Two were in the Pacific, and two in Europe. While in the Pacific, my uncle Charlie even received a medal for decoding enemy messages on his radio. He continued to tinker with radios even after the war. I liked visiting him in his basement flat. He seemed to genuinely like my company even though he was somewhat of a recluse. Sadly, he never shared his experiences of the war.

In the United States for a couple of generations, my family went through the Great Depression. While these were hard times, we were fortunate to own a grocery store. I have wonderful memories of all the delicious salamis and sausages hanging up with the mozzarella balls all tied in a row, and barrels filled with delicious pickles and olives. My parents always made sure we had the freshest produce in the area, getting up every day before dawn to go to market. They worked hard and assured their clients the best for their money.

With summer coming along, I was getting bored and wanted more than working in the family grocery store. I knew it would make my father happy if I stayed on, but I was still serious about joining another military outfit. He just didn't understand that the most excitement here in our neighborhood was outrunning the gangs of bigger guys who tried to rob me of the money I earned while working at the grocery store or on my shoeshine route. I might have been able to fight a couple of these thugs, but not a whole gang! It was getting even more dangerous when I put out the trash behind the grocery store and found guns tossed in the garbage can! Crime was on the rise in the city. The police were having a hard time keeping up with the incidents. To me, this was reason enough to get away.

On my birthday in June 1950, my friends and I marched down to the Marine Corps recruiting office and made the decision to join. Nothing was going to change our minds.

We were told that we had to pass a physical, but I wasn't worried since I was a fit runner and a featherweight boxer. The obstacle proved to be the written test. We didn't get to finish and were told to come back the next day.

As we left, we saw the Army's recruiting office next door and, with desperate determination, my friends and I went in and joined!

My dad wasn't pleased but he wisely let me take responsibility for my actions. He quietly drove me to the bus station so I could head out to Camp Dix, New Jersey, for basic training. I met up with a couple of my friends there.

How naïve we were, thinking this was going to be fun!

Foolishness and impatience can get young people in trouble. If only we had been paying attention to world events!

The Korean War began June 25, 1950. Little did I know that my life would be forever changed.

I was welcomed with the brutality of the officers in boot camp. I can only describe them as rabid as dogs. Since this camp was once used as a prisoner of war camp for Italian prisoners from World War II, any Italian was treated like an enemy. Only four or five years had passed since the war and animosity and antisemitism hadn't worn off. I now understood why my grandparents rarely went out for fear of Italian haters.

One officer stood apart for his sadistic actions. "Little Jesus," as we nicknamed him, thought he was a god and accountable to no one. I remember when he ripped off our gas masks during a training maneuver. He threw the masks where we couldn't retrieve them. Toxic gases filled the sealed room we were in. Some of the new recruits frantically broke windows to get fresh air!

Already tall and slender, I now looked like a scarecrow since I lost a lot of weight during boot camp. My parents tried to fatten me up when I returned home on leave after basic training.

After returning to base, I was given an assignment for tank training in Fort Knox, Kentucky. I was attached to Company B, 33rd Medium Tank Battalion of the 3rd Armored Division (the same one that Elvis Presley joined). One of our duties was to guard the vaults of Fort Knox. I had visions of seeing stacks of gold, but that was only a dream.

Aside from the normal shenanigans that happen in any army camp, this time was memorable only in the friendships developed with other fellows my age. Too soon we would all find ourselves with orders for deployment to Korea, a place none of us knew of. We had no idea what awaited us.

Psalm 25:7 – "Do not remember the rebellious sins of my youth. Remember me in the light of your unfailing love, for you are merciful, O Lord."

Leaving from Seattle, Washington, we sailed the Pacific Ocean crossing the "International Date Line." (This is the imaginary line that goes North and South through the Pacific Ocean. One day is on the east side of the line and the following day is on the west side.) A certificate was issued to each of us, as a memento of the crossing.

Sailing on an old war ship named "USNS *Marine Lynx*" took us about 20 days. Wintertime and seas were rough and made me grateful I was not in the Navy anymore. We landed first in Japan, then were ferried over to the port of Pusan, Korea.

Korea, "land of the morning calm," is a peninsula that projects south from Manchuria, China, about 500 miles, with widths ranging from 125 to 220 miles. Someone mentioned it was the size of Minnesota and just as cold. I thought it looked more like Florida covered with mountains, which take up about 85 percent of the land! Whatever is flat was used for rice paddies, while valleys carried rushing water.

The extreme freezing temperatures shocked us, as much as the lack of food, clothing, and ammunition. There was nothing calm about this place!

My memory lapses again from the time I landed in Korea and the train ride out of the port of Pusan. I recall bits and pieces, much like spliced film. Only the changing of the seasons, the personnel of soldiers around me, and history hold a clue as to how events unfolded.

I think it was during our short visit in Pusan that I traded my $20 watch for cash to a South Korean merchant. Had I stayed around, I'm sure I would have learned some choice Korean words.

Reaching an Army assembly area in the north for assignment took at least a week. The trains weren't able to continuously run as scheduled. Tracks were blocked by enemy activities or the mass exodus of Koreans moving south. There was no other way for us to travel north.

Delays would open up gaps in defensive lines if replacements couldn't arrive to reinforce the dwindling allied military forces.

I remember it was below freezing and we hadn't even reached the northern part of the country! I had never experienced temperatures reaching below -30 degrees Fahrenheit.

As we were getting ready to load up from the train station platform, I saw a tiny Korean boy. His ears were turning a dark purple from being so cold. On impulse, I tossed him my pile cap. It was said that many of the guys who were known never to share, offered their last morsel of food or hats to children. Compassion was catching.

It would be a long time till I was issued another cap or get clothes to keep me warm in this weather. Opinion was that we would get this job done, and be home for Christmas. I sincerely hoped so because I was freezing!

As we rode a windowless boxcar heading north, I remember being cramped together. We could only stand up.

Suddenly, loud noises like rocks banged against the side of the cars and broke the monotony of the train ride. Someone shouted.

"Grenades are bouncing against the sides of the train!" The train lurched to a stop.

"Jump out. Prepare to shoot!"

My adrenaline pumped full force. The moment became a frenzy!

The skirmish didn't last long. We scattered only to get ambushed by a large number of enemy soldiers. We didn't know what to expect. Meeting the enemy face to face, holding guns up to our faces, we quickly assessed what we were up against. Their weapons were like none we had ever handled. They looked warmer and more adapted to this weather, dressed in what looked like quilted bedding from their coats down to their leggings.

Within moments, shouts and threats erupted!

Thousands of enemy soldiers surrounded us. (As documented in the "Second Division history book", the train ambush took place between Taegu and Wonju by a superior enemy force making its way to meet American lines the first week in January.)

An American voice said, "Surrender! Hands above your heads! They'll shoot us dead!"

Even though this could have been a Chinese soldier since many had been to American universities before the war and spoke perfect American, no one questioned the order.

2 Samuel 22:2-59(NKJV) "The Lord is my rock and my fortress and my deliverer! The God of my strength in whom I will trust; My shield and the horn of my salvation and my stronghold and my refuge; My Savior, You save me from all violence! I will call on the Lord who is worthy to be praised; So shall I be saved from my enemies. When the waves of death surround me, the floods of ungodliness made me afraid!"

About 20 of us were taken captive from the train and marched into the hills. As time went on, more prisoners joined our ranks till we totaled near 200 men.

I noticed enemy soldiers started dispersing, leaving behind approximately 800 to surround us. The idea that we could try to overtake them was suicidal. I quickly dismissed that thought!

I did my best to make myself small and inconspicuous among the prisoners. The ploy hardly worked as we got shoved, kicked, and beaten. The North Koreans enjoyed using their rifle butts as they passed us. Some of the prisoners had their hands behind their backs with barbed wire twisted around their wrists. I wondered if they had tried to escape.

Marching up and down hills for many hours, I wasn't sure if we were still in South Korea or had reached North Korea!

At dusk, our captors finally stopped at what appeared to be a layover camp. Nothing looked permanent except for deep holes in the ground. We were shoved into these holes, alone, and caged in with bamboo hatches overhead.

Extremely exhausted, hungry, and cold, I just wanted to sleep. An overwhelming sense of survival forced me to stay awake. I had heard about the brutality of the enemy and needed to be as alert as possible. (Close to three of every seven Americans taken prisoner died in prison camps).

When I didn't hear any voices or enemy patrols during the night, I decided to escape. Now was my chance! I didn't want to die here.

I pushed my body against the bamboo hatch, literally crushing my skinny bones through the openings, to pull it apart. I chewed at whatever resisted. Mustering up all my strength, I squeezed through.

Psalm 121:2-8 – "My help comes from the Lord, Who made Heaven and earth! He will not let you stumble; the one who watches over you will not slumber. The Lord Himself watches over you! The Lord stands beside you as your protective shade. The sun will not harm you by day, nor the moon at night. The Lord keeps you from all harm and watches over your life. The Lord watches over you as you come and go, both now and forever."

I clutched at fistfuls of dirt and lifted myself out. I knew I would need backup and couldn't escape alone. Crawling over to the next hole, I whispered to the soldier there.

"You want to make a break for it?"

"Yeah! Where is everybody?"

"Shh," I pleaded.

Given hope, the soldier silently joined me by tugging hard on the hatch. It was so tight pulling the hatch apart, the soldier almost got strangled. Luckily the captors didn't find my "P-38" can opener, a small metal rectangle of one-and-a-half inches that laid flat along with my dog tags. It has a sharp hook when unfolded. I began shredding at the bamboo.

It seemed to take forever but he finally slipped free. Now we could hear voices stirring. There was no time to approach other prisoners. My hope for them was that we would make it back to friendly lines and send a rescue party out.

It was night and we were in the dark. Which way to go? I noticed then that the young soldier was looking up at the stars. He signaled me, pointing. As silently as our heavy boots could take us, we ran up and down hills. For sure we were "under the shadow of the Almighty"!

Psalm 25:15 – "My eyes are always on the Lord, for he rescues me from the traps of my enemies."

Near dawn, we finally reached American lines. It looked like the entire Eighth Army was in a circle. I ran up and started shouting to everyone I met, "I just escaped!" I was directed to several officers, till finally a Master Sergeant told me to report my information to the Red Cross Station. I was told someone there would relay an order to the proper rescue party. I never saw the other soldier again, nor did I hear of any rescues.

Once my report was done, I headed over to listen to guys on a podium declaring the virtues of joining the "Second Indianhead Division." I raised my hand and was told to move to the right. I liked their motto, "Second to None." They had a beautiful insignia of an Apache Chief over a large star.

On one of the days that followed the assembly area, a ceremony presentation took place. The loud speaker announced, "Order Arms!" I noticed all the other soldiers stood at attention with M-1 rifles. Until now all that was issued to me was a 45mm pistol. I yanked it out.

While I was holding it skyward, a shot rang out. I stood shocked! Commotion began and someone bellowed, "Get that man, now!"

The General ("Ruffner," I believe) was none too happy! Some soldier came, grabbing for me. Almost knocking my helmet off, I pulled away and shouted,

"Don't touch me!"

Turning and addressing the General, I said,

"I'm sorry, it was an accident, sir! The chamber must have misfired!"

His response was not quotable! Then with a change in tone, he added, "Look here, this is what you should have done!"

He proceeded to show me the method of cocking a pistol without firing it, using his 45mm. This covered a humiliating situation and turned it into a productive lesson, for which I was grateful. Though officers could take profanity to an art form level, these were the men others followed into battle. Leaders with Bibles safely tucked in field jackets and not afraid to be seen reading them or showing kindness instilled devotion to duty and country.

Soon after the presentation ceremony, we would face the blow of battles to come.

Matthew 11:28 – "Come to me, all of you who are weary and carry heavy burdens and I will give you rest."

Sal on leave

Ft. Dix

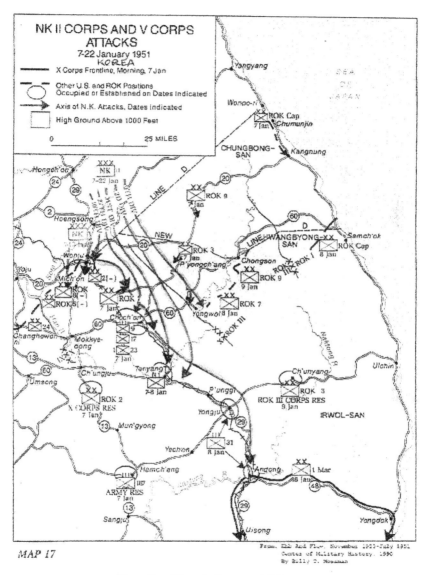

Map of positions in January 1951

MAP 17

JOURNEY'S END

As we are approaching the end of this voyage, I want, on behalf of the ship's personnel and myself, to express our sincere gratitude to all officers and enlisted men for your superior discipline and co-operation in respect to the ship's regulations.

This voyage was rough and consequently the holiday season was not enjoyed by you as much as it could have been under more favorable weather conditions.

But fortunately in your group there was such a large percentage of talented persons who contributed a lot for entertainment and they are highly to be complimented for their Christmas gift to us.

Happy landing to all of you and may God's blessing guide you in carrying on your honorable duties.

Vernon Lans
Master, the Marine Lynx

* * * * * * * * * * * *

"They that go down to sea in ships, that do business in great waters; these see the works of the Lord and His wonders in the deep" and ..., "so He bringeth them unto their desired heaven. Oh, that men would praise the Lord for His loving kindness, and for His wonderful works to the children of men!"

NEWS
SOUVENIR EDITION

VOL. I NO. 13   FRIDAY, JAN 5, 1951

As we come to the end of our voyage, the words of the 107th Psalm come readily to mind. Most of us never realized just how "big the ocean is" until you tried crossing it on a 16-knot transport. But as unending as the vast reaches of the ocean are, the Lord is greater still. "If I take the wings of the morning, and dwell in the uttermost parts of the sea; even there shall Thy hand lead me and Thy right hand shall hold me." (Psalms 139:9,10).

I believe we have seen the "works of the Lord" and his "wonders of the deep" during our trip together. God has brought us thru safely and we are grateful. And many of you have come to know Christ in a new and living way as your Saviour and Lord. Hundreds of Bibles and Testaments have been requested, showing a renewed interest in the Word of God. And as your chaplain it has been a privilege to be with you, and your attentive support of the worship services has been a distinct encouragement. May your appreciation understanding and enjoyment of the things of God deepen as you face new and dangerous assignments.

To the faithful newspaper staff, the librarians, the choir and all the men who assisted in the many details to help make a "happy ship", a hearty "well done!"

For all of you, God's blessing, protection and a prayer for a safe and soon return to home and loved ones.

W. B. Leonard, Jr.
Ship's chaplain and
editor.

(Other messages on Page 3.)

Newsletter from Marine Lynx

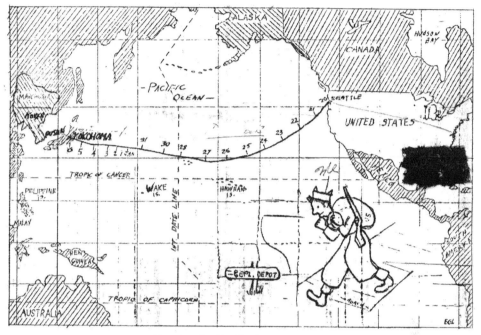

Crossing the Pacific Ocean to Korea

CHAPTER 2

War Makes Men Out of Boys

I will say of the Lord, "He is my refuge and my fortress;
My God, in Him I will trust."
~ PSALM 91:2 (NKJV)

It seemed like months had passed, but my next memory happened only a few weeks later.

While on a scouting mission through a village, I found what looked like a sewer cover. Lifting it, I spotted charred remains. These turned out to be bodies of captive G.I. soldiers. (The bodies looked charred because blood turns black when frozen; these men had been frozen to death).

I ran and reported back to my Sergeant who ordered me to go down into the hole to collect a dog tag from each body. I was scared to go down in a dark hole with all these dead men. It was eerie touching them while getting the tag from each soldier. If I let my mind wander, I could almost imagine one of them reaching out to touch me. Refocusing on the job at hand, even though I wanted to rush out, I made sure to leave the second tag attached on the chain for each corpse. I felt like I was down in the pit forever.

The collected dog tags were turned over to our Commanding Officer so the identity of each soldier was documented. The importance of this did not slip my mind, because later I would regret not knowing the names of many of the brave soldiers who were taken prisoner with me or died alongside me in the war.

The killers were long gone from this deserted village. We continued searching an enemy that was cunning, deceptive, and attacked in large numbers like a massive wave of humanity. It destroyed in its wake.

"Operation Killer" had begun. My designation as a soldier, MOS, was changed to rifleman.

Psalm 27:2-5 "When evil people come to devour me, when my enemies and foes attack me, they will stumble and fall. Though a might army surrounds me, my heart will not be afraid. Even if I am attacked, I will remain confident. The one thing I ask of the Lord – the thing I seek the most – is to live in the house of the Lord all the days of my life, delighting in the Lord's perfection and meditating in His temple. For He will conceal me there when troubles come; He will hide me in His sanctuary. He will place me out of reach on a high rock.

The enemy had snipers everywhere. Infiltration was their biggest tactic. They preferred to sneak into our camps at night, slipping into foxholes and stabbing our sleeping soldiers. Our blankets were taken away so we wouldn't get too warm and sleep soundly. The consequences of not staying alert, especially while on outpost duty, could be serious damages to an entire battalion or company! Despite having passwords and questioning any strangers, it was still easy for the enemy to pretend to be our South Korean allies, the ROK Army. Many Chinese officers had studied in elite schools such as Harvard before returning to their homeland. Their English was flawless. It was like fighting your best friend. I could not let my guard down over sentiments.

"McCune" and I were promoted to Corporal at the same time. I thought he was an old man by the way he spoke and the way he walked. Just like a big country boy from Oklahoma, he always had a wad of chewing tobacco in his cheek, which made the mole on the side of his mouth look like a fly. He would say to me, "Come on now, Mac, I'll take care of you. I'll show you how to shoot!"

Opportunity came when I spotted an enemy sniper behind a tree. "McCune" turned to me and said, "Where's the enemy? Should I get 'em or do you wanna try?"

I had already aimed my M-1 rifle and started shooting at the tree. Side to side, back and forth, I emptied my ammo clip. The tree resembled a frazzled Christmas tree. I continued shooting more rounds and as I was about to reach for a new clip, another soldier shouted, "Enough! Enough! He's dead and you are using up all our ammo!"

"I didn't see him fall," I replied.

"You probably have him stuck to the tree with all the splinters you made," the other soldier answered.

We encountered many enemy patrols as we made our way through the valleys in the vicinity of Hoengsong. This town is located almost in the center of the Korean peninsula. Southeast is the town of Wonju and due west is the coastal port of Inchon.

A lot of planes napalmed the area to rid large concentrations of the enemy. We witnessed one of the planes crashing into the high mountains. It was probably weighted down with bombs so heavily that it was incapable of lifting its nose properly. The huge explosion could be felt throughout the valleys and the large plume of black smoke was spotted miles away.

As we moved into February, I remember being near the Command Post of our unit. I was waiting to get food prepared by "Popeye," our company cook. He was a thin, scrawny-looking man with a week's beard and a corncob pipe in his mouth. My mother always said, "Don't trust a skinny cook," but Popeye always dished out a warm, tasty meal. We were grateful for him since this was a rare treat and quite a change from our usual frozen C-rations. Normally we warmed our canned rations by storing them in our field jackets in between battles.

It was then we heard an eruption of shooting and fighting above us on a nearby hill. Looking up we spotted enemy soldiers. Dropping everything, we ran while drawing our weapons!

Halfway up the hill a sniper shot a soldier. As he came tumbling down past me, I recognized him! It was "LaFevre"! (He was reported killed in action, KIA, on February 4, 1951). I knew him as the hairy, burly looking guy from Indiana who sailed with me to Korea on the "Marine Lynx." We always seemed to be at cross purposes or swinging at each other. I guess we did this as a way to let off steam in close quarters. I was shocked to learn that he was my age! He seemed older. At just barely eighteen, I thought everyone looked older than me.

I remember he called me "Wings." I was so skinny that I was able to pull my shoulder blades back in a weird way, making me appear to have wings. It grossed out many of my friends. Sergeant Nick remembered me as "Scarecrow," running up and down hills. Others called me "Bones."

To see a person you know die brutally in front of you makes you do much soul searching. I couldn't believe it! I now understood the saying, "War, in the passing of just seconds, makes men out of boys!"

Psalm 3:3 - "But you, O Lord, are a shield around me; you are my glory, the one who holds my head high."

I then heard Popeye coming up behind me, shouting,

"I'll show you youngun's how to get this done right! I'll get 'em!"

The sniper was still around and firing strong. Marching up the hill, Popeye had become the prime target. He went down without another word! I managed to run over to check on him before the stretcher bearers could haul him off.

"I'll be back," he said in his feisty tone of voice.

I was glad he would be all right! A lot of company cooks got shot and killed since they were normally close to the Command Posts targeted by the enemy in their attempt to ambush the Company Command and seize records, along with any vital information they could put their hands on. This accounted for the fact that many of our army records were destroyed before they fell into enemy hands.

Another reality check! This was not target practice at boot camp! No blanks here! You cannot miss the clarity of war: life or death, kill or be killed!

I had to turn away from the wounded and somehow reach the top. On a side hill I saw a Sergeant standing in front of a hut where an old woman was sitting cross-legged. I could vaguely hear him speaking to her. Pulling out a gun from her covered lap, she shot him! I yelled out to her, warning her to drop her gun! She still held her gun ready to shoot. I aimed and fired. I shot her, but it was too late to help the officer. Shooting a woman, even though it was war, bothered me for a long time. We had to kill the enemy attacking, regardless, but it still went against my inner beliefs of never hurting women.

Artillery opened up at that moment, hitting the hut and causing a couple of enemy soldiers to jump out. They were Chinese, identified by a red star pinned on their caps. Their uniforms looked clean cut and tailored fit. That definitely set them apart as officers and from the North Koreans with more rugged pile caps and outfits. I shot at them, but was forced to retreat down the hill, away from their returned barrage of fire.

When I reached the bottom of the hill, I encountered another Sergeant giving orders. He directed two of us to go to the opposite small hill. We were to look out and stand guard for any enemy sneaking up behind our company. The young kid that accompanied me was blond, tall, and slim, weighing about 185 pounds.

We immediately spotted two Chinese snipers as we reached the crest of the hill. Turning to the young soldier, I pointed out the difference in their uniforms with the visible red stars on their caps. The snipers ran for cover into another straw hut.

I nudged the kid and said as quietly as I could,

"Throw your hand grenades."

"I'm only sixteen! I'm turning myself in! I'm going to tell them I want to go home!"

I couldn't blame him. He was probably one of those kids from larger families who signed up for combat pay and lied about their age.

Forcefully, under whispered breath, I said, "Throw your grenades!"

Together we threw our hand grenades and blew the hut to pieces! One enemy soldier crawled out and I shot him. There were no other enemy sightings, so we reported back to the Commanding Officer.

Sometime later, I looked around for the kid, but he was gone and no one seemed to know him or remember him. Hopefully he was able to go home.

The Second Indianhead Division continued on the move. We passed along a ridgeline where, a couple of months before, the battle of "Kunuri Roadblock" took place. (From November 26-29, 1950, the U.S. Eighth Army's advance towards the Yalu River was cut off by strong enemy attacks. Communist Chinese forces initiated a fast encirclement and pursuit operation.) This battle was conducted in extreme freezing temperatures and over rough terrain, cutting off our allies from vital support and communications. Only a few of our troops were able to withdraw and escape annihilation.

We could still see the signs of chaos that took place. Body parts lay preserved by the bitter cold, amidst overturned trucks and tanks, broken everywhere! It was a difficult scene to march past. This is a cold and cruel country! I said a silent prayer.

Psalm 34:18 – "The Lord is close to the brokenhearted; He rescues those whose spirits are crushed."

Despite the bitter cold, perspiration formed in boots and on beards, turning to ice. Damp socks meant frozen feet. Our bodies were taxed to the limit with knee-trembling, steep climbing.

We walked loaded down with our own supplies of weapons and necessities. The water in our canteens froze. If not engaged in battles, carbines and automatic rifles had to be fired every half-hour or so, to keep them from freezing. We would field strip and reassemble our weapons clean every day, when possible. We got so good at doing this, we could do it in one minute, even in the dark, when necessary. *When possible* and *when necessary* became words that we told ourselves like a mantra. One day at a time, one hour, one minute, is all you can handle.

Our bodies got little care. Stress, lack of food, and no personal time kept us from even doing nature's calling. No one could bear pulling their pants down in this freezing weather, so we would just shake our pant legs out quickly!

A more troublesome effect of this icy climate was reported by the medics who couldn't administer vital solutions to the wounded or sick because the tubes would clog. Blood froze on wounds before it could coagulate.

Against the Siberian frigid winds, tanks were pushing aside as much of the road blockage made up of broken or disabled military vehicles, as they could, to allow for new convoys to pass. We were on foot, behind the tanks that also shielded us from the piercing wind. We also saw the remains of many dead enemy soldiers abandoned alongside the road, frozen just as they died. One of the tanks in the lead of the convoy got too close to the edge of the cliff which started to crumble under the weight. The tank toppled over quickly down the hill, end over end. Watching in horror, I started running after it in order to help the tankers. As I was about to climb down the embankment after the tank, I was grabbed from behind.

"Don't go. They won't need help now."

Sorrow was becoming my constant companion. Accepting death was not easy and I could only take refuge in prayer. "God, please rest their souls in Heaven. Amen."

John 16:33 – "I have told you all this so that you may have peace in me. Here on earth you will have many trials and sorrows. But take heart, because I have overcome the world."

CHAPTER 3

Roadblock, Rampage, and Repression at Hoengsong

Surely He shall deliver you from the snare
of the fowler and from the perilous pestilence.
~ Psalm 91:3 (NKJV)

Sometime around the beginning of February 1951, I was designated ammo bearer to "Hogan", having been assigned to the 60mm mortars of "C" Company, 38th Infantry Regiment of the Second Indianhead Division.

I thought Hogan was also from New York because he had an accent. There are so many nationalities in the neighborhood of Brooklyn, New York, where I was born. This made for a melting pot of people, creating different dialects and languages. Some were Jewish from various countries, Italians, Irish, Puerto Ricans, and many Asians, including Chinese. I quickly assumed Hogan was from my neck of the woods and thought that was why we got along very well.

Since he had been fighting in Korea for months, I figured he must know a thing or two about soldiering and survival. Actually, Hogan was from the bayou country of New Orleans, Louisiana. We both had pitch black hair and stood about equal at five feet eleven inches. What set us apart was that I was a feather weight at 125 pounds compared to his 170 pounds.

I shuffled along in boots that were way too big for me. Blisters formed all over my feet. Every step was painful. The additional weight I had to carry didn't help. I carried my mortar's 40-pound base plate, plus the mortar rounds which were fitted like a saddle bag front and back over my head and fastened. Suspenders held bandoliers of ammo clips for my 9-pound M-1 rifle, and my 45mm pistol. Then to top all that, we carried rations, poncho, blanket, field jacket, helmet, and boots, all total weighing over 125 pounds! My skinny legs and feet had to carry over 250 pounds!

Hogan hated my complaining (which he remembered 50 years later)! My whining didn't do any good because as foot soldiers we were expected to carry our weight, trudging up and down hills till our legs buckled and our feet bled!

Aside from this, we partnered well, and our operation of sending mortar rounds was done with precision. The rounds had to be called out in numbered charges. "Two," "three," "four!" I would pull out the charges he called for and throw in the rounds and fire. He would pull his field glasses out and view the target. "We got them!"

One evening we were told to dig in for the night because large numbers of enemy soldiers had been spotted. It took a while to dig because the earth was frozen. Just as Hogan and I were finally climbing in, a sudden burst of tracers came across the top of our heads. The firing was intense!

"The Chinese must have overtaken our guys in the upper positions, because only our troops have tracers. Let's get out of here!" he shouted.

All hell broke loose as we reached a lower position! Hordes of enemy soldiers were coming at us like a giant wave! I kept firing my M-1 rifle back and forth, emptying the clip.

"Hogan, Hogan, I see them coming! What should we do?"

Darkness was camouflaging us so we stopped firing. We didn't want to give our new position away. The enemy was so close.

It wasn't long before we heard voices echoing, "Hogan, Hogan!" The enemy scare tactic unnerved Hogan!

"Don't call me Hogan!"

He got up and ran. I followed him. Enemy fire rounds erupted and pushed us down the hill to a road. The battle was intensifying. I had emptied all my clips. I had no choice but to use my 45mm pistol.

Running along the road, I spotted another M-1 with a clip and picked it up. Within minutes I was out of ammo again.

The Chinese and North Koreans were coming from all sides. Trucks, tanks, soldiers, everything in their path was blown up! There had to be at least 240 tanks and 90 trucks lying in broken heaps or sitting disabled. It was chaos! American tanks that weren't disabled were shooting point blank at the hills or trying to clear out a path to escape the roadblock.

Psalm 3:6-7 – "I am not afraid of ten thousand enemies who surround me on every side. Arise, O Lord! Rescue me, my God! Slap all my enemies in the face! Shatter the teeth of the wicked!"

(this scripture brings to mind the story Sal told about when the enemy were found dead after a battle, silver teeth were scattered on the ground. There was so much silver that the young allied soldiers started picking them up and stashing them in their pockets. At some point Sal got spooked and threw away all that he collected).

The screaming and hollering were overwhelming. The violence of battle explosives and wounded men's cries tear at a man's soul. Darkness offered me cover as I tried to hitch a ride on the side of a tank. It appeared to be moving out. I ran after it and tried to reach the box with the phone but I couldn't budge it open. I don't know why it seemed important to do this. Maybe some of my tank training was kicking in. The guys inside had to know I was hitching a ride. Surprise and scaring them would lead them to open fire on me. I'm not sure I was recognizable as an American anymore because of all the dried blood and dirt that covered me. I finally flung myself on the tank, only to find there was someone already there. I was face to face with an enemy soldier! We both stared at each other, shocked for a split second. My adrenaline was pumping furiously. A combination of fear and a strong will to live pulsed through my ears. I felt an overwhelming sense of super strength. Taking the advantage, I leaped on him, grabbing him by the throat.

I growled. Years later this experience returned as a flashback. I remembered and actually cried out, "Ow! He bit me!" This enemy soldier had bit me on the arm, hard enough to draw blood!

We struggled and both fell off the tank to the ground. Grabbing him, I shook him, expecting that he would fight me again. All I held was a limp and seemingly lifeless soldier. I wasn't sure why. Did he get shot? Did he break his neck falling? I'll never know. There was no time to check if he had been wounded. I was exposed out in the open road and needed to find cover, quick!

Looking around I spotted enemy soldiers on both sides of the hills and running along the road. As I ran, I spotted a bugle on the ground. I reached for it, only to have it snatched out of my grasp by an enemy soldier. The moment was surreal to me, like I was running along the streets of my neighborhood, evading the bullies trying to steal my wallet. Blasts of shooting brought me back to my senses.

Suddenly an Army truck appeared ahead of me. It seemed to be carrying dead soldiers. I made a mad dash and jumped on, burrowing myself under the bodies. I heard some moans. There were soldiers still alive! I could then hear the distinctive thud of bullets hitting flesh. An enemy sniper had zeroed in on me. I peeked through the bodies around me and saw a Chinese soldier throw a concussion grenade under the back of the truck I was in. Within seconds, the truck was lifted up by the explosion and I was propelled into the air. I felt my body fall back to the ground with a flop, like a wet rag. Body parts were raining down on me. I passed out.

When I regained consciousness, still dazed, I shook my head, hoping to clear it. I don't know how long I had been on the ground. The chaos of battle, machine gun fire, burp guns, bugles, and all the cacophony of war was still going on. Panic hit me. I was in hell!

As my head cleared, I refocused on safety. I automatically got up and started running. I didn't take time to wonder whether I had been wounded, despite being drenched in blood. If I could run then I was alive! I picked up an M-1 and bandoliers abandoned along the road. I started pumping shots continuously in the direction of the largest enemy group.

At the break of dawn, I spotted another of our trucks moving away from the slaughter. Another soldier joined me as I jumped on the back. Relieved he was not an enemy, I waited till we were at a safe distance from the gunfire, reached up, and tapped on the window. It would be the worst irony if the driver and his passenger shot us, not knowing they had two American passengers in back. We laid down as flat as we could because machine gun fire began hitting parts of the truck.

I woke, not realizing I had passed out. I didn't hear any battle noise. We had managed to evade the enemy and been driven to an Airborne medical field tent. A doctor examined me and found blood coming out of my ears, telling me I had a head concussion. I had no idea what a concussion was. To me it meant a giant headache. As it turned out, seizures, tremors, and humming in the ears were going to be just a small part of it!

It was probably the heavenly bliss of being in a warm tent, feeling safe, that allowed me to sleep on a cot, stretched out, oblivious to the world around me. I was alive and warm, thank You, Lord!

Psalm 4:8 – "In peace I will lie down and sleep, for you alone, O Lord, will keep me safe."

I was awakened by an officer asking if pancakes, eggs, and sausage sounded good. Was he kidding? I couldn't remember how many days it had been since I'd eaten even a cracker!

As I sat down at the table along with the other fellow that rode with me, I started shaking uncontrollably. My hands were rattling so bad. The officer bent down and asked, "Are you all right?"

He turned to the other fellow and asked him, "Is he always like this?"

"I don't really know him, sir," the soldier replied.

I ate everything on my plate, piled high with food, despite my shaking hands. Sated, I was then allowed the luxury of going back to sleep. Much too soon I was awakened again by the officer. Time to regroup with my unit.

"Can't I stay here for a couple of days?" I asked.

"Wish you could, but I have my orders. Your unit is waiting for you," he replied.

It was close to evening and would be dark soon. After calling in to First Battalion headquarters to let them know I was coming in, I was flown out in a Piper Cub close to their location. The remaining couple of miles from the combat zone, I was trucked in. From there, I was given orders to head out and walk towards the bridge that was scheduled to be destroyed. I would find the 38th Infantry nearby. They sent me off with a wish of good luck.

All alone I skirted the sides of the mountain to avoid land mines. The havoc created by these mines could be seen all along the trail. I finally found a group from the Second Division. One of the Captains spotted me and yelled, "Where in hell have you been? We'll talk later! Go find your men or someone you recognize!"

I looked around and saw no familiar faces. It seemed like a long time before I would see Hogan again. (From morning reports, "Hogan" would go on R&R on February 25). I joined with those wearing my Army patch and was back to the fighting.

During the following day, February 12, "Baker" was running near me. I knew him from boot camp. We were trying to outrun some enemy soldiers. Gunshots rang out and he was thrown to the ground with blood across his back. I drew up next to him, reaching for him, and he started shouting, "Run, buddy, run! Save yourself!"

I managed to pick him up, carrying him across my back, and we somehow managed to dodge bullets from enemy soldiers. It was a miracle we made it to an evacuation truck. At least he was in safe hands. I prayed his wounds weren't severe.

When Baker was taken to a hospital, he met up with another friend of ours, "Vinny." Baker told him what happened. Vinny knew my folks and was corresponding with them, so I found out Baker had pulled through okay. Vinny mentioned they both had to learn how to walk again. After Baker's wounds healed, they designated him as a company cook. Vinny's letter of April, 1951, recorded when this all happened.

I later learned that the Field Artillery Battalion had been ambushed, which is how the enemy had a chance to overtake the higher positions. The 38th Infantry suffered 530 men killed at Hoengsong.

Psalm 18:29 – "In Your strength I can crush an army, with my God I can scale any wall."

HEADQUARTERS, 38th Infantry
APO 248, c/o Postmaster
San Francisco, California

SECRET

NARRATIVE SUMMARY

for

February 1951

The period of 1 February opened with the 38th Infantry occupying positions in the vicinity of WONJU with the mission of patrolling extensively to north.(1) The 3rd Battalion disptached a company size patrol to the northwest and upon nearing the vicinity of the lake, DS 039415, encountered a large enemy force and became heavily engaged. Artillery and air was placed on the enemy with excellent results, numbering an estimated 63 KIA. Reports from members of the patrol indicated that the enemy was well disciplined and trained. While artillery and air was being placed on his positions, the enemy would take cover in his fox-hole. Immediately after the fire was lifted he would resume his firing position and continue to deliver fire on friendly forces.(2)

During the morning of 2 February, the 38th Infantry received orders from division to secure the high ground just north of Hoengsong. Division further directed that one Bn would be prepared to move west of HOENGSONG to the SAEMAL area to establish blocking positions on the QQ line.(3)

The 3rd Bn, leading element of the RCT, followed closely by the 1st Bn, departed for HOENGSONG. At 022330, both units closed into their assigned areas. The 2nd Bn, minus "F" Company, utilizing the transportation used by the leading elements, arrived at HOENGSONG at 030500. "F" Company remained

Secret report Feb. '51 for 38th Inf.

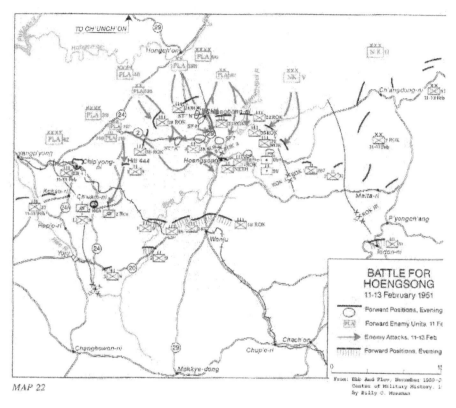

MAP 22

Map battle for Hoengsong Feb.'51

CHAPTER 4

Promotion, Perception, and Pork & Beans

He shall cover you with His feathers, and under His wings you
shall take refuge; His truth shall be your shield and buckler.
~ PSALM 91:4 (NKJV)

We reassembled after the roadblock to reorganize our battalions of the 38th Infantry around the town of Hoengsong. The battle became familiarly known as the "Hoengsong Roadblock."

This battle had the most concentrated loss of American lives after the battalions of field artillery were killed in an ambush. (From February 11-13, 530 men of the 503rd and 15th Field Artillery, not including 2,018 casualties of the 2nd and 7th Infantry Divisions and the 187th Airborne.)

"Augie" was wounded on February 13, as well as "Willie," who was sent to a MASH and was eventually evacuated home to the United States.

Following the major enemy thrust in the roadblock, another strong enemy force was seen on a ridge nearby. They wasted no time sending in heavy barrages of mortar rounds and firing burp guns on our troops.

The fighting was so intense that soldiers were getting that blank stare look or having nervous breakdowns. To alleviate these symptoms of emotional numbness or burnout causing ineffective combat, the military set up two measures: one was R&R, the other was Rotation. I remember Sergeant Zegedy going on R&R around February 6, 1951. Since I started combat in January, I looked forward to my turn. Length of overseas duty depended a lot on how close one was fighting to the front lines. The tour was set up on a point system and one had to earn 36 points to go home. Infantrymen rated four points per month. I served over 12 months. I can't imagine why I was there so long or whether they took away points for being wounded. I think on average most of the soldiers served 10 months.

Another incident around this time happened when one of the "Bande" brothers of "C" Company became seriously wounded. When his brother rejoined the company group and heard the news, he went crazy. Shouting and screaming, he grabbed his rifle and began shooting in every direction. He snapped, thinking his brother was dead. A large cook called "Big Red" came running out to help get the situation under control. The cook had to smother him till he passed out. It was the only way to subdue and stop him from getting hurt or hurting others. Last I heard the brothers were both evacuated.

Around this time, we were being led by "Chief," our Major. He was one of the bravest men I ever met. I later learned that he was one of our country's most decorated war heroes, having served in three wars –WWII, Korea, and Vietnam. He was a paragon amid our division, retiring from his Army career as a Lt. Colonel with five purple hearts, 22 combat wounds, along with the Distinguished Service Cross, two Silver Stars, nominated for the Medal of Honor in WWII, and considered for one in Korea.

We nicknamed him Chief since he was a member of the Maidu Indian Tribe, from an area called Black Hawk. We had a lot of Native

American Indians in our division. Perhaps the Indianhead on our insignia influenced their selection in joining the Second Indianhead Division. They were exceptionally noted for scouting out the enemy. One of them told me it was easy. Just follow the garlic smell on the trail because the odor gives away their presence. The enemy have it in their food and it permeates their bodies. I worried afterwards since I ate spaghetti with garlic in it. I didn't want to be a target.

I was promoted to PFC, private first class – 3, along with Walter, Baker, McCuen, and Gourley. This was stated on Morning Reports of February 9, 1951.

One particular day, I had the honor of fighting alongside Chief when we were ordered to assault the nearest hill held by the enemy. Typical warfare in Korea was fighting for tactical hills.

As we were shooting at an enemy machine-gun nest, I spotted two enemy soldiers running towards us. Both wore navy blue clothing, re-sembling a dark T-shirt with baggy slacks. I took aim and shot them, killing them both instantly. It was still painfully unnerving and per-sonal to shoot the enemy face to face. Looking at another human being I've killed, most of them just boys looking younger than myself, haunts me. "We chose for you the fortune of war rather than a shameful peace. With breaking hearts, we bowed beneath the stroke of fate ..." (From a speech by Stephen Lee from around 1863, in New Orleans.)

The day was very cold and my M-1 bullet clip jammed. The soldier next to me tried to unjam it while I used his gun to give us cover. Spotting another M-1 lying on the edge of a bomb hole about five feet away, he said to me, "Go get that one! I need mine!"

Since it was too dangerous to be without a weapon, I crawled over the ridge towards the hole. I noticed one of our soldiers was killed there with a dead enemy soldier beside him. Saying a quick prayer, I left because of the fighting and regretted not being able to get his name.

After I picked up the abandoned rifle, I also noticed a couple of dead enemy officers nearby. There was a leather briefcase beside them. I inched my way over and retrieved it. I also spotted a beautiful bone-handled pistol. Collecting all the items, I scrambled back. Making my way to Chief, I turned over the briefcase to him, and kept the pistol. My pistol was long gone, so this was a blessing.

The battle raged on and we kept shooting to keep the enemy from taking any ground. We overtook and held the ridgeline.

No more than ten feet away, down the hill, I noticed a guy having traumatic convulsions. I remembered his name as "Gilbert." Someone had put a pencil in his mouth so he wouldn't bite his tongue. He had a big chin, but a skinny face.

About the same time, another soldier from our group walked past us like a sleepwalker in a daze. I remember he had black hair, but now it was white as snow! The soldier next to me said,

"Look, that's what fright does to a person!"

Considering the fragile condition these guys were in, I wondered if anyone was going to collect and remove them from combat, out of harm's way. Later I found out that Gilbert was taken prisoner. (According to casualty reports, Gilbert was captured and taken to North Korea. He would be a POW till the end of the war. He was returned to U.S. Military control on August 21, 1953.)

While in a prone position, I was still firing the M-1 picked up back on the hill. I found myself next to Chief, with my elbow almost touching his leg. He must have gotten up to view the ridge with his field glasses. Suddenly, he spun around and tumbled backwards. I got up and ran down the hill to see if I could help him.

"Go back up there on the ridge and help them fight. I'll be all right. The aid men will be here shortly!" he yelled.

Obediently, I went back up the ridgeline where our company was holding the hill. Throughout the action, mortars were raining down on us. Finally, the remaining enemy was pushed back into the mountains.

Covering the enemy retreat was a small Chinese tank with a red star on it. It had come out of the woods and aimed directly at us. One of our soldiers ran towards it but stumbled, wounded by an enemy soldier in the turret. We gave him overhead protection. Although hit, he managed to pull himself up and lob the grenade. The tank exploded and lay disabled. No enemy soldiers came out.

Later when I met up with Chief, he told me that the can of pork and beans he had in his field jacket saved his life! The bullet pierced the can and superficially grazed his skin. I vowed then that no matter what I carried, there would always be a can stored in my field jacket.

He also mentioned the briefcase I found during the battle, saying he had delivered it over to his superiors in Command. One of the officers found the documents very important because they showed that the Chinese had maps detailing our locations. Chief thought that I would probably be awarded a medal for retrieving the documents and being observant while under fire. I was thinking this would make my mom proud of me.

A newspaper article by combat correspondent Connie Sellers recorded how Chief finally submitted to medical treatment after the hill was secured. A medic told how he reacted when nearby firing increased: "The Major jumped up off the litter, grabbed his carbine and took off for the fighting again!" (According to the *Casualty Book of the 2nd ID,* Chief was wounded February 12.) The Chinese counterattack involved 18,000 enemy troops. In the Wonju/Chipyong area, three U.S. divisions participated: the 1st Cavalry, and the 2nd and 7th Infantry Divisions. (From February 12-21, we suffered 651 killed in action and 1,296 wounded).

On February 16, "Kappus" was sent to the 121 Evac. Hospital. As badly wounded as his legs were, he would come back months later to fight with us again.

Deuteronomy 28:7 – "The Lord will conquer your enemies when they attack you. They will attack you from one direction, but they will scatter from you in seven!"

Battle at Hoengsong

CHAPTER 5

Grievous Deeds, Guardian Angels, and Gentle Giants

You shall not be afraid of the terror by night,
nor of the arrow that flies by day.
~ PSALM 91:5 (NKJV)

We moved out again to cross the Han River and retake Seoul.

Our first big challenge was the river at sub-zero temperatures! Getting wet was to be avoided at all costs. Frostbite was a strong possibility but since we had no pontoon boats or rafts, we rode on the sides of Army tanks.

It became evident very quickly that when the water reached the tank tracks and splashed water all over our legs, getting wet was unavoidable. Within seconds, our pants were frozen like boards! We became numb. My feet froze in soggy boots and the hair on my legs came off. Our only good fortune at this particular moment was that the enemy had not attacked.

There was a Captain in our company whom we nicknamed "Socks." Never knew his real name. He was strict about making us change our socks so our toes wouldn't freeze. He threatened to court martial anyone who didn't obey! We were instructed to keep one pair warm and dry tucked inside our field jackets and to exchange our worn ones once they became sweaty or wet.

I really thought I would never be warm or dry again!

Retaking Seoul meant we encountered heavy enemy units and were engaged in battles every day. My unit, First Battalion of the 38th Infantry Regiment, closed in on the vicinity of Chadong, while the 1st Ranger Company successfully raided an enemy force in the village of Changmal.

After a battle I came across a fellow soldier lying on the ground, wounded in the throat. I bent down to help him, putting my hand under his head, laying it on my lap. Blood was pulsing out of his throat. I put pressure against it with my hand.

He kept moaning, "Food, food!"

Reaching into my bag, I found a C-ration can marked spaghetti. I opened the can with my P-38m can opener, chopping the frozen meal to make small pieces. I used my fingers to feed the wounded soldier. He had such a grateful look for the meager bits and pieces.

Then I noticed food was slipping out of the hole in his throat. Before I could act on it, I was jerked up by the back of my jacket!

"Come on! We have to move fast!"

I must have had a hesitant look, because the officer said,

"The medics will find him and help. Let's go!"

I relented but really felt bad about leaving the wounded soldier all alone. It was probably "Szegedy" who pulled me away. As my Sergeant, he always seemed to be looking out for me. My guardian angel, Sarge was a World War II veteran, maybe in his late thirties, a little over six feet tall, with a roughened-looking face and black hair.

During another battle, the enemy pushed us into rice paddies. We trampled over the patchwork of these water-logged areas, taking cover as best we could. I crouched down against a mound of dirt. That's when I found a beautiful, shiny brown lacquered box, about the size of a shoebox. I called out, "Hey, look what I found!"

Upon closer inspection, as I was getting ready to pick it up, I noticed wires dangling from it. With my arms still outstretched toward the box, I could hear Szegedy speak with a stern voice.

"Do not touch that! Back away! NOW! Slow and easy!"

He had come up alongside me and when he saw the box was still on the ground, he slapped me across the head! Then, he showed all of us the wires running around everywhere. The rice paddy had been wired and the box was the detonator that would have sent off charges, blowing us all to pieces!

"Clear out!" he ordered.

Thank God for these World War II veterans in Korea. They had the maturity and experiences of war that were necessary to keep us young ones alive.

Proverbs 4:5-7 "Get wisdom; develop good judgment. Don't forget my words or turn away from them. Don't turn your back on wisdom, for she will protect you. Love her, and she will guard you. Getting wisdom is the wisest thing you can do! And whatever else you do, develop good judgement."

There was another incident when I found a small enamel box filled with powder. When I went to smell it, a hand slapped it out of my hand, and the powder flew out like dust. Szegedy later explained it was opium, commonly used by the enemy foot soldiers.

By now we had become like scavengers because we were so hungry. I resorted to eating coffee grinds mixed with some snow. This was also around the time we didn't have enough to drink. The water was poisoned in many rivers and streams so we couldn't refill our canteens there. The enemy targeted our food drops and killed anyone who dared approach the drop site to retrieve the crates of supplies.

Our many encounters with the enemy led us to exhausting our supply of ammunition far quicker than what had been calculated. We never had enough ammunition, food, or water at hand.

I was so ravenous I would eat the little rice balls left behind after a battle by dead enemy soldiers. The rice was mixed with a bit of fish paste and garlic. It didn't taste good but it was better than starving. This must have been confusing to our company scouts trying to trail enemy soldiers by sniffing them out. No one ever said anything to me. Court martial orders were for drinking any ground water or wearing the warm quilted clothing of the enemy soldiers.

At one point I must have still been starving because someone gave me a cigarette and said,

"Here, this will help!"

So, I ate it.

"You stupid idiot, you were supposed to smoke it!"

(During the wars it was believed that smoking was a way to keep hunger pangs away and also a relaxant.) The hollering must have been by Szegedy.

Around this time while our company was walking through a deserted village, we found an abandoned cow. The barber of our company, probably "Bell," killed and butchered it. He always had the sharpest, well-honed knife in the entire regiment. This was the first time I would taste "Beef Tartare." After starving for so long, I didn't care whether I liked it or not. This may account today for my preference of eating meat well done!

Once we left the safety and cover of the deserted village, advancing on enemy locations in an open area required walking behind a tank. The rice paddies weren't safe, but being behind a tank was no better. The lead tank got blown up on a land mine. The enemy had zeroed in on us and continued their open fire directly on the remaining tanks. We scattered for safe positions. As I moved along a berm, I spotted a couple of enemy soldiers and fired back while they were exposed, but in doing so I exposed myself! Sure enough, a hand slapped me across the head again.

"Get down you, stupid jerk! You want to get killed?"

As we made our way into another little village that was still burning from the air strikes and bombs sent in to flush out the enemy, I recall Sergeant "Moose" was with me. We gave him this nickname because of his deep, almost bellowing voice. As we looked for cover and shelter for the night, we spied a hut on the outskirts of the village that had escaped the napalm drop. The heating ventilation was ingenious in this hut as it distributed the heat from a wood-burning stove through channels under the floorboards. On a cold winter night, this would be more than comfortable. Of course, we couldn't build a fire for added warmth, but the ground was sufficiently warmed by the bombing outside earlier.

I was ordered to take shifts every two hours at an outpost. There went my dream of staying warm! I was grateful Moose accompanied me. It was scary in the dark with eerie noises. The cowbells jingling and owls hooting were especially creepy. I turned to Moose, asking, "I'm scared, aren't you?"

"Sure, I'm scared. My shorts aren't yellow because I bought them that way," he answered.

This made me feel better. I wasn't alone. At least here was a World War II veteran who was smart enough to be scared and was honest about it. On the other hand, Moose may have been ordered to make sure I went and stayed on "picket duty." Too soon I was instructed to be on outpost duty alone. There came the owl hoots and the cowbells again!

My ears were on high alert. Then I spotted someone coming towards me. "Halt!" I said.

The figure still came. "Halt or I'll shoot!" No answer.

Isaiah 21: 8-9 "Then the watchman called out, day after day I have stood on the watchtower, my Lord. Night after night I have remained at my post. Now at last, look! Here comes a man…!"

55

By the silhouette, I finally made out the figure approaching. He hollered, "It's me, you jerk! Can't you tell the difference between me and an enemy soldier?"

I was thinking, what happened to passwords? We had Babe Ruth, Jane Russell, or Clark Gable. Any of those would have worked for me. I shut up and said nothing because he was coming to take over my place, thank God!

To keep warm another evening, our group bedded down in a haystack at an abandoned farm. The next day we itched so bad with lice and vermin that we could hardly hold our weapons. Because of all the scratching we did, we looked like cats had jumped and clawed us. I remember a truck came out to the fields, ordered us to strip down, get sprayed, and dusted with some sort of powder. Our clothes were so filthy and infested they were heaped for the burn pile. Maybe this is when we finally got white parkas, to blend in with the snow.

We were cleaned up just in time because we soon found ourselves in a skirmish. Machine gunners had zeroed in on us. We actually had to fall back. I kept firing my rifle, back and forth, but soon realized there was no one firing alongside me. Realizing I was facing the enemy alone, another quick look around also told me I was on the edge of a precipice and the jump would be at least thirty feet to the ground. With the enemy hot on my heels, I had little time or much choice for decision making. I jumped. Somehow, I avoided getting hit from behind, but landed on my own rifle, with my shins across the barrel. I crawled away in pain while shots were hitting the snow-covered ground around me! I finally made it to a safe point and limped into the area where my unit had regrouped. The gashes across my legs were bleeding. I hoped I wouldn't need stitches. The material of my pant legs soaked up the blood and there was no time to get medical aid. I would forever have dents on the front of my legs.

Psalm 18:39 – "You have armed me with strength for the battle; You have subdued my enemies under my feet."

I found out that Szegedy had been wounded. He would have made certain that I was given the chance to get first aid or at least clean bandages for my legs. Szegedy was wounded in the face. Luckily the bullet caught him at the corner of his mouth and ran upward around his head, like a backward letter C. His wound did not injure his head or eyes or any vital areas. His stitches later looked like a burn mark, a scar he probably carried the rest of his life.

Before I could miss him more, he came back to the front lines to fight alongside us until he rotated home weeks later. He called me over before he left and handed me a paper with his address on it. I'll never forget his parting words to me.

"Come down and see me, ol' buddy. You're okay for a Yankee!"

Sadly, the paper with his address got lost in the shuffle of battles to come.

It was around the beginning of March, 1951, that I was promoted to Corporal along with "McCuen", "Walt" and a couple of other soldiers in our Regiment. (Documented by the morning reports).

1 Corinthians 15:57 – "But thank God! He gives us victory over sin and death through Our Lord, Jesus Christ."

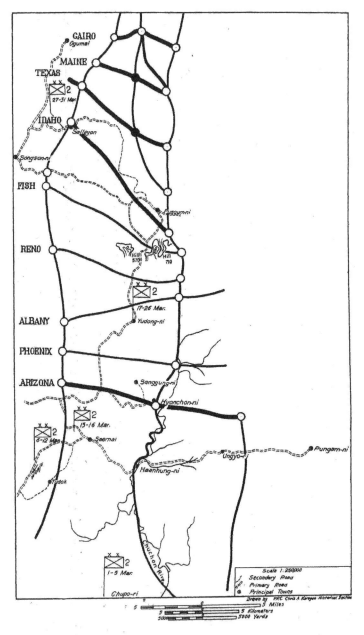

Named Lines March 1951

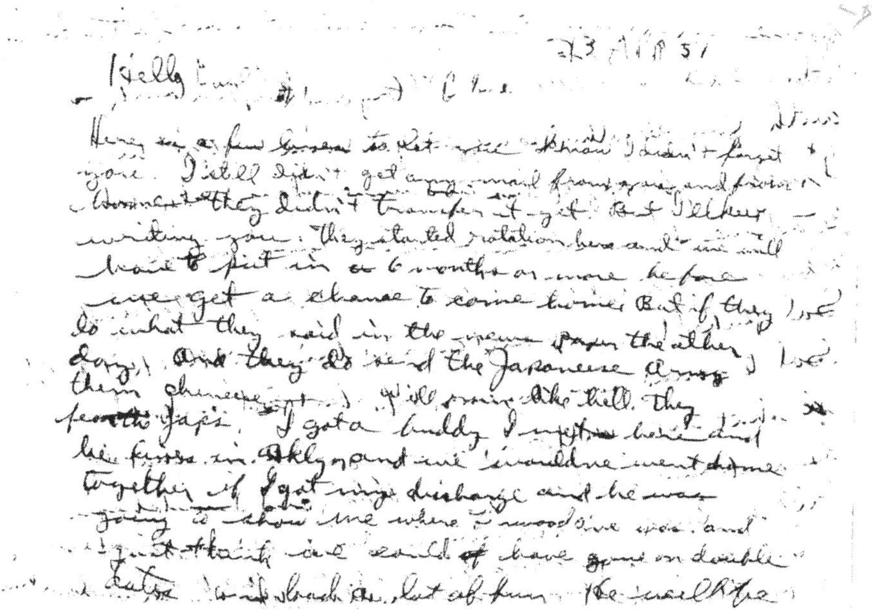

Hello [illegible] 23 Apr 51

Here are a few lines to let you know I didn't forget you. I still didn't get any mail from you and from home they didn't transfer it yet. But I'll keep writing you. They started rotation here and we will have to put in 6 months or more before we get a chance to come home. But if they do what they said in the newspaper the other day, and they do send the Japanese Army [illegible] them Chinese [illegible] will run like hell. They fear the Japs. I got a buddy I [illegible] he lives in Bklyn and we would have went home together if I got my discharge and he was going to show me where [illegible] and I just think we could of have gone on double dates [illegible] a lot of fun. He will be

Vinny's letter

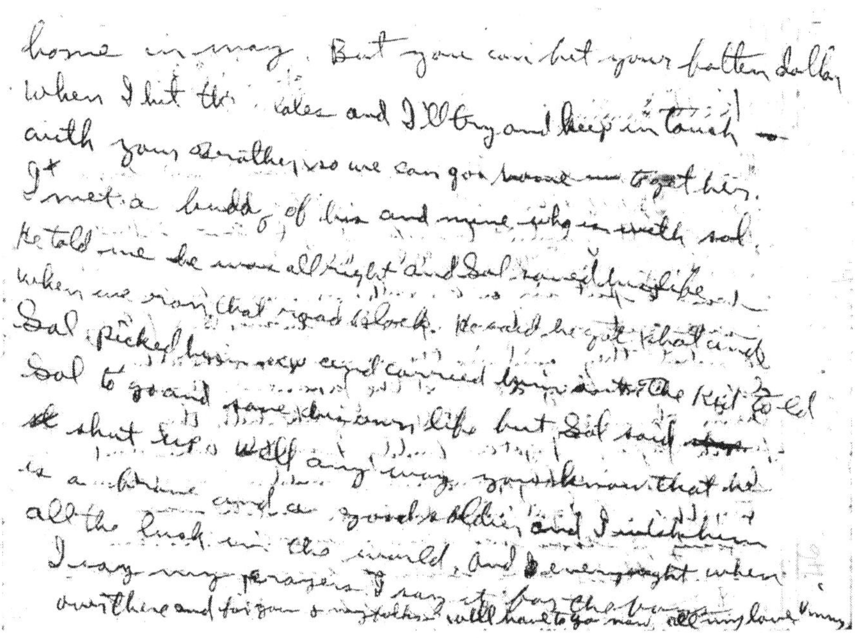

home in May. But you can bet your bottom dollar when I hit the states and I'll try and keep in touch with your brother so we can go home together. I met a buddy of his and mine [illegible] with Sal. He told me he was all right and Sal saved his life when we ran that road block. He said he got hit and Sal picked him up and carried him [illegible] shut up. Well any way you know that he is a [illegible] and a good soldier and I wish him all the luck in the world, and [illegible] every night when I say my prayers I say it for the boys over there and for you & my folks. Will have to go now. All my love Vinny

Vinny's original letter

Smoke from exploded mortar shell

Taking cover in a ditch

Litter bearers improvising

CHAPTER 6

Turks, Thirst, and Tootsie Rolls

You shall not be afraid … of the pestilence that walks in darkness,
nor of the destruction that lays waste at noonday.
~ Psalm 91:6 (NKJV)

I would have many reasons to be grateful this day.

Another battle began. We always seemed to be exposed to the enemy and needed to take cover. I spotted a bunker with four openings. Deciding it looked safe, I ran towards it, and dove in through one of the openings. Imagine my surprise to find it occupied by an enemy machine gunner who was silently sitting there! Lucky for me the gun was aimed in the opposite direction and he couldn't swing around fast enough to shoot me! Faster than the blink of an eye, I leaped out of there! No more than thirty feet away from the bunker, I could hear the machine gun fire erupt. The gunner had me in his sights, shot me in the legs and continued to fire away. He was determined not to let me get away, judging by the barrage of fire he sent my way. My legs were on fire! I dropped and rolled while lobbing a hand grenade backwards.

Psalm 27:1 – "The Lord is my light and my salvation – so why should I be afraid. The Lord is my fortress, protecting me from danger, so why should I tremble?"

I kept rolling down the hill until I thought I was safely out of range. Standing up, I had another surprise. I found myself in the middle of a Turkish brigade. These soldiers looked scary and menacing with their dark looks and big moustaches. Self-preservation makes one do some instant evaluation. I quickly recognized them as the group attached to my 38th Infantry. I ran up to the biggest fellow in front, shouting and gesturing. "Up hill. Chinese!"

One of them pointed and said, "Show."

Despite my bleeding and hurting legs, I lead them back up the hill to the now silent bunker I had just escaped. We crept up to it cautiously. It was apparent my grenade had hit its target. We were out of harm's way for the moment but had to be careful because the enemy was quick to replace strategic points that targeted us.

"Okay, okay," said the big Turk. Patting me on the back, he called over some of the other Turkish soldiers and they began exchanging words. Of course, I couldn't understand them or figure out what they were saying.

The pain in my legs was nothing compared to the now overwhelming need for water. I felt parched and so thirsty. We hadn't been able to drink or eat in a long while. My tongue had swollen once already from lack of water. We couldn't drink from any streams or water tanks because of the fear of dysentery. Our Sergeant had given us some pills to put in our own pee and drink the solution. We did this as a group, since most of us thought that this was disgusting and that we were really going to be poisoned. Doing it all together didn't seem so threatening. We asked ourselves: the Sarge wouldn't kill all his men, would he?

I had hoped never to have to experience that again, so I wasn't shy about asking the Turkish soldier for a drink. I was given a bottle. Thinking it was water, I took a few good gulps. I kept drinking a few more swallows and handed the bottle back. Almost instantly my throat felt on fire! The stuff I drank was so potent, it burned all the way down to my stomach. Now I really thought I was poisoned. I choked and coughed. My eyes were tearing up. The Turkish soldiers seemed confused at my reaction. They left without a word. I unknowingly may have insulted them. Later maybe, while sitting around their campfire thinking on it, they may have had a good laugh at my expense.

When I rejoined my company battalion, I heard some stories about the Turks, especially their method of baiting the enemy. At night, they would set up their campfires, making their own meals. They didn't like the canned rations we received when we did get some. Maybe the fact that we didn't get food regularly added to their reason for fending for themselves. I remember them appearing as though they were on a camping field trip! They would talk loud and generally make as much noise as possible. They were letting the enemy know where they were. Meanwhile, they would have the other part of their group hiding in the bushes or behind rocks, waiting for the unsuspecting enemy who thought to ambush them. For me this strategy seemed suicidal and probably accounted for the higher number of Turks getting killed.

I heard another story circulating about "The Tootsie Roll drop." Some of our ammo was nicknamed "Tootsie Rolls." We received our ammo and food by air drops which usually offered the perfect situation for the patient enemy to ambush us. Some starving soldiers lost their lives trying to reach food. When an order for more ammo was placed, the air drop that followed was sent in several crates. Much to the surprise of the Artillery company, the boxes contained real candy Tootsie Rolls. That would not have helped in defending our positions! I could just imagine if the enemy had opened these. The enemy would think the Americans were losing it. I'm sure the Chinese that lived in America prior to the war were familiar with the candy so this would have really been perplexing. However, there was a mixed blessing to this story. Someone came up with an ingenious secret. After chewing the candy till it was soft and pliable it was used as caulking in the armatures that had cracked due to the freezing temperatures. Once exposed to air the candy became rock hard and sealed the cracks. Armature that would have had to be discarded now was able to function, at least until the hot weather came in.

I would always write home as soon as I could catch a break. My mom saved my many letters and gave them to me when I got home. I was so distraught at the time and overwhelmed by the effects of war that I wanted no reminder and burned them. Little help that did since my nightmares and flashbacks were daily reminders. I regret getting rid of the letters because I'm sure there were names and places, or even events, that I have forgotten.

Recounting some of the funny little stories to my mom helped her not to worry about me too much. After writing about the bunker incident, she sent me back an article that made it in our New York newspapers: "Soldier is fast to jump in and out of a bunker, occupied by the enemy!" The news correspondent from the *"Stars and Stripes"* wrote the article after our interview at the "38th field aid station" when I finally got the bullet fragments taken out of my legs.

Interviews with soldiers telling their experiences in battle were received by a public information officer. I'm thinking that not many stories made it home. The public back home didn't want to know about the gruesome details of war. Or because many of the correspondents, photographers, and filming crew were prime enemy targets, much of their material was lost. Mostly what we have is actual footage or photos from the enemy.

The American photographer Douglas Duncan was a great photographer who managed to print many of his photos of the Korean War in a book.

The infirmary was not like you see on *MASH*, the television show. It resembled a campout, no tents, and many wounded laying out on stretchers on the open ground. The medics tried their best to get intravenous drips going, hoping the cold didn't freeze the plasma or antibiotics. Medics would have to step over bodies that were in so much pain and fighting hypothermia from the hard, frozen ground. These wounded soldiers didn't care as long as the medics could dose them with ampoules of morphine, which were often in short supply due to the amount of war casualties.

After my legs were patched up, I was sent back to my battalion on the front lines again. My legs would have to carry me a lot farther because we were told to get geared up and out for some heavier retaliation from the enemy!

I wrote my mom that I was getting promoted and moving up the ranks quickly. I was made a Corporal and I might come home a General if the war lasted any longer! I'm sure she got a good laugh out of that.

I was learning not to look back at what happened but to keep focused on the moment. The immediate present time happening, always anticipating, always moving, always geared up, that made the adrenaline always pumping a mile a minute, depended on focus for survival!

Proverbs 3:21-24 – "My child, don't lose sight of common sense and discernment. Hang on to them, for they will refresh your soul. They are like jewels on a necklace. The keep you safe on your way, and your feet will not stumble. You can go to bed without fear; you will lie down and sleep soundly."

U.S. casualties reached 157,530 in the three years of hostilities.

US ARMY PHOTO

38th Infantry aid station

CHAPTER 7

May Massacre Mayhem

A thousand may fall at your side, and ten thousand
at your right hand, but it shall not come near you.
~ Psalm 91:7 (NKJV)

The events of May are like spliced pieces of a film, randomly placed together, and out of sequence.

(I had to compare my notes with Army records, letters from other soldiers or their families, morning reports, battle reports, Second Division history book and the Second Division Casualty book.)

On May 10, 1951, "McCracken" wrote home. We were all told to write home because our company was waiting for orders to move out for an attack on Chinese forces reported to be in large numbers and heading towards our Indianhead Division lines. It would be his last letter home to his mom and twin brother. McCracken and I were together since basic training. We took a lot of pictures back then. The best memory is his crooked smile, like he was hiding a secret. Easy going, he always went along with whatever our group was planning.

"Annihilate the Second Indianhead Division!" These were the orders passed down from the Chinese High Command that were intercepted. Their "Spring Offensive" was to completely envelop the American Eighth Army and destroy it. One news article read, "Chinese Commissar plauds 2nd Division, as the best division in the American Army." Another article stated that they were seeking revenge for the devastating losses they had suffered earlier in the year.

First Lieutenant "Welch" was wounded in the ankle on May 12 while we were walking along a ridge. I picked him up and, putting one of his arms around my shoulders, we sought out a safer position. When evacuation trucks for the wounded came nearby, we moved out to approach them. It wasn't long before some shrapnel flew in, completely shearing off the whole front of my field jacket. Stunned, I looked down, and realized my hand grenades were ripped off too!

Welch glanced over at me. "Phew! You're lucky!"

I can only say, God saved us both that day.

Psalm 118:13 – "My enemies did their best to kill me, but the Lord re-cued me."

Nearer to the trucks, Welch spotted some soldiers shooting. They were too close for comfort and he blurted out, "Dumb bastards! They'll wind up killing us!"

Shouting out passwords to the surrounding soldiers and the truck drivers, I was finally able to help Welch climb safely into a truck. Once I saw it was rolling out, I returned to my platoon.

On May 15, another one of my best friends from basic training, "Maybin," was wounded seriously in both arms and legs. I was told a mortar round came in on him. He was evacuated and later sent to Hawaii.

The Sergeant who always watched out for me, Szegedy, was wounded on May 16.

"Augie" was in a foxhole on May 17 when a concussion grenade landed near him and took his leg off. Not able to crawl to safer ground,

Sergeant "Matteo" went back and pulled him out. The soldier next to Augie was killed instantly. Matteo received an award for his bravery.

I witnessed First Lieutenant "Camp" shot in the head. I reported him killed in action.

As we were climbing "Hill 1051," preparing for battle, I spotted Sergeant "Clark" sitting on a rock, taking deep gasping breaths. I stopped to ask him, "Are you all right?"

He was breathing so hard he could barely talk. "I have asthma," he gasped.

I tried to encourage him to move on, but he just couldn't take another step. I had to catch up to the remainder of my group, so I resumed climbing up the steep hill. It wasn't too long after that I heard machine gun fire in the distance. As I turned around, more shots were fired and I saw Clark fall down. They later told me he was killed. (Casualty book dates this May 18).

What was a schoolteacher with severe asthma doing on a battlefield, not to mention climbing the rugged terrain of high mountains? I questioned the Army's judgment then, because surely he would have better served the war effort behind the lines, working on the tons of reports at headquarters. At least then our records would not have been such a mess.

Matthew 5:9-10 – "God blesses those who work for peace, for they will be called the children of God. God blesses those who are persecuted for doing right, for the Kingdom of Heaven is theirs."

I was sent out on a reconnaissance with four or five others on May 18. We were patrolling to locate enemy positions. I heard mumbled voices. An officer with me leaned over and whispered, "Don't make a sound. Let's turn back. We're being surrounded! When you hit our lines, run like hell!"

Out of nowhere, "Lovin," another friend from basic training who joined Company K of the 38th Infantry, came running over the hill shouting, "Run, buddy, run! They're coming!"

Our group scattered just as mayhem broke loose! Bugles, screams, loudspeakers, bright lights, bombs, machine gun fire, and explosions erupted! It was so deafening it made me want to crawl in a hole with my hands over my ears and make everything go away.

Walt, who was on a different scouting mission, said that the biggest Mongolians he had ever seen attacked them and shot "Hoppy" in the stomach. Seeing him fall down, Walt thought he was dead.

Lovin was carrying an 80mm gun. He earned a bronze star for running ahead of the enemy, warning the units, and for retrieving the gun before the enemy could grab it. At the bottom of the hill, far from the fighting, was a group of officers handing out medals. I guess that was as far as they would go to see that medals were distributed. Like free day-old bread, first come, first served.

(I had sent away for some reports of the 38th Infantry, Regular Headquarters, that were labeled "Secret." After 50 years, they released them. It was stated that awards were being sent back to Headquarters because the intended parties could not be found, either due to death or capture, or they had been evacuated due to wounds. The reports go on to state that this was unacceptable, and that all efforts had to be expended in handing out awards.)

By now our area was invaded by hordes of enemy soldiers spread apart in numerous columns, and running over the hills like armies of ants. This was to become the battle of "May Massacre."

"Victor Terry" was called in. Artillery shells were exploding across the ground. Over the PA system, the loudspeaker was booming, "Fight to the last man!" Soon after, the voice came back on yelling, "Strategic withdrawal!"

We were forced to our secondary positions, about 100 feet lower down the hill. From this place, I spotted Sergeant "Moose" and Captain "White" get captured. They were on the opposite side of a horseshoe shaped ridgeline from me. I could see the enemy surrounding them. They must have done something to Moose because I heard him bellow out a fierce growl! I was so afraid for them. I tried to shoot as many of the enemy as I could.

The enemy captured Hoppy who was critically wounded. (Hoppy's wife would later write to me that if it had not been for one man in the prison camp who was willing to incur the wrath of the captors, her husband would not have survived. That man tended to Hoppy's wounds and fed him portions of his own ration, meager as they were!)

Sergeant "Kappus," an older soldier from Wisconsin, was shooting from a bunker we were both in. Positioned right alongside me during the battle, he was shot in the forehead. He had told me he was engaged to marry a nurse back home. Here was someone else that should not have been fighting because his wounded legs were still raw from an earlier battle. They looked like bad stitching on a football. All the climbing we had done in previous days had split his stitches wide open. He had fresh blood soaking through his pant legs. Even if his life depended on it, running was not an option.

As I jumped into a safer hole, I spotted McCraken about three holes away. Two holes away were Sergeant "Banks" and Second Lieutenant "Two-Gun Mairich," who sported two pearl-handled forty-five caliber pistols in his two-gun chest holster. Sergeant Nick, who had joined our company about a week before this event, often kidded that if anything happened to Mairich, those guns were his. When Mairich was carried out days earlier on a stretcher, he whistled over to Nick, with one hand on his chest over his two guns, and with the other hand raised he waved the finger. I guess they patched him up quick too because here he was in this battle with us!

I shared my new position with a soldier, a Czech named "Slachta." He had a strong build, and would pound his chest proclaiming that he was "Nick." He had blue eyes, dirty blond hair, and his nose was always red, like someone who blew their nose a lot.

Our hole was larger than most because it had a stash of hand grenades and ammo cases. We were near a large rock on our left, and artillery hits made it look like fireworks. Fourth of July fireworks, except this was May!

The enemy came over the hilltop, running towards us. I started lobbing grenades. Slachta was screaming, "Don't throw the grenades! They'll spot us!"

They knew where we were. They were coming right for us. The ammunition was there to take out as many as we could before they reached us. I was good at launching grenades. The enemy scattered and scrambled for cover. I continued throwing grenades. Even though darkness now provided the cover I needed, I could still see enemy silhouettes running towards us. Unnerved, Slachta got out of the hole and ran down the hill.

Soon the enemy was blindly following him, jumping in and out of my hole. They must have thought he was alone because no attention was given to me. I easily pretended to be dead since I was covered deep in blood from all the bodies killed. By the glare of weapons being fired, I could detect the leg wrappings that the enemy wore. They were literally stepping on me now. More bodies were falling. There was so much blood, I thought I would drown in it.

I had to make a run for it or be discovered by returning enemy soldiers. They would backtrack and start shooting all the bodies lying around to make sure they had killed us. I had to wait for the right moment. As I patiently bided my time, the sky lit up from the overhead bombing. I saw a cliff about 150 feet away. That would be my objective.

Lifting myself out and running as fast as I could, I followed the cliff down the ridge. I couldn't see much and got stuck in some bramble bushes. One of our soldiers was nearby and cut me loose. (I believe this was a Ranger, attached to the 38th Infantry.) Together, we made our way farther down the ridge and spotted some men walking towards us. At first, I thought these were our men coming to join us. The other soldier grabbed me and lifted his finger to his lips for silence.

These soldiers were Chinese and there was an army of them coming! We took cover, scrambling as quiet as we could, back into the bushes. The Chinese columns marched right past us, single file, for hours, right into dawn's first light! (Here was my nightmare. Hiding in the bushes, holding my breath, as enemy soldiers walked past).

We found out later that several Chinese units totaling close to 200,000 soldiers had flanked us from the rear and were moving in to secure "Hill 1051."

They raised the Chinese flag when they reached the summit. It rankled to see the red flag with a large gold star surrounded by four smaller ones on it. Our American flag had been there that morning! The Ranger and I moved out and ran to reach American lines. The Chinese on top of the hill spotted us and began firing. I could feel pellets hitting my back.

"Don't worry. We're out of range from their guns. The bullets are falling short," my companion said.

We continued at a fast pace down the rest of the hill and came across annihilated American tanks and artillery gunners. These were the guys that helped us with "Victor Terry" the evening before. Many pieces of artillery were blown up and many dead men were draped over the barrels of the guns, stripped of their clothing and armament. The smoke was still lingering.

Returning to our friendly lines, a Captain gave the order to regroup. After recording the men present, someone mentioned to me that only seven men were left standing from my Company C! Since a company usually had about 150 men, that meant we were missing almost 143 men, either wounded, killed, or captured. Some would be called MIA, missing in action, because their bodies were never accounted for.

The captain gave orders to march back up the hill that coming night. We were to take back "Hill 1051." That left few hours to recoup from exhaustion and hunger, so it was best not to argue.

I received a field promotion to temporary Sergeant. To keep that position if I survived the war, I would have to take a test when I reached stateside. Walt remembers following me up that hill, later in the evening as I directed the men. I was "Point Man."

Big trucks with flare lights lit up the entire hill. The battle would begin again. I was shot in the head and evacuated to a hospital in Osaka, Japan. I don't remember anything about being shot or evacuated, though I did wake briefly on a cot alongside the fuselage of a plane. Sergeant Nick told me years later that he was the one who found me in a hole. Thinking I was dead, he was about to put me in a body bag. As he pulled me out of the crater by my suspenders, he heard me moan. I had to have lain there a long time, possibly a whole day, since only after the battle does the body bag platoon go out to gather the dead. Nick figured that I must have been knocked unconscious by an incoming mortar round, and the Chinese came through the battlefield and executed all the bodies lying there. My helmet was shot point blank. I escaped with shrapnel in my head. Years later Nick drew my portrait with the hole in my helmet, as he remembered it.

I woke days later, in a hospital with a purple heart medal at the foot of my bed. I blacked out again because when I woke next, I heard soldiers in a fierce argument. I was now in a hospital ward with other soldiers. Some were Army, some were Marines. They were blaming each other for not being supportive and evading their duties, chickening out, or who were being cowards! Words and insults were flung around! Feeling a maelstrom of emotions, I found myself in the middle and began defending the Army. When a doctor came in doing the rounds, he quickly targeted me because I appeared to be the troublemaker with a lot of fight in me. He said I could get my head checked in the States later.

"You there! You seem to be in top form! I have determined that you are able to be returned to duty!"

I now felt like a fool! I had a hole in my head, and my brains felt like marbles rolling around. Why didn't I just stay quiet, for a few more days of rest? (Morning reports show the hospital stay was for ten days total. Records stateside would try to state six months in the hospital, but morning reports and battle reports validate the days and locations of service.)

It became apparent that there were not enough men left to engage the enemy in Korea. They needed anyone they could get, even those with holes in their heads!

Upon returning to duty, I asked where my battalion men were. Sergeant Nick was wounded days after me, as well as McCuen and Walt. I was glad to hear Hammer was not killed but wounded in the leg. I witnessed him falling down in his hole and enemy soldiers jumping in. He later said that he pretended to be dead. Hogan was rotating home. McCracken and Mairich were captured and died of their wounds. McCracken's twin brother fought the army to get him his purple heart. After 50 years, his mother was ceremoniously presented the award by their state Congressman. (His brother did not live to see it).

Hoppy and White would come home after the war, released from captivity. Augie was evacuated back to the States because he lost his leg. I found out years later that he had never received his "Purple Heart" medal, "Combat Infantry Badge" or any recognition for his service. Members of the 38th Infantry, Korean War Association group, vouched for his service with evidence from records obtained and testimonies. Unfortunately, Augie passed away before the medals could be awarded him.

On May 24, 1951, General Omar Bradley revealed in his testimony the terrible, updated cost of the war (most of the speeches were reported by the *"Stars and Stripes"* news, at that time. Without a doubt this could not have included the many casualties of the May Massacre battles). American battle casualties were noted at 69,272, which included 13,349 missing in action, MIA, or captive. Non-battle casualties, including dysentery, frost bite and such, were at 72,679. Ten enemy divisions had flung themselves in an all-out attempt to annihilate the

2nd Indianhead Division. Another two communist divisions followed after to probably be used as occupational forces. It was a major defeat for the enemy, losing an estimated 300,000 men!

Isaiah 27:1 – "In that day the Lord will take His terrible, swift sword and punish the swiftly moving serpent, the coiling writhing serpent. He will kill the dragon…"

SUBJECT: S-1 Evaluation for period of 1 May 1951 thru 30 May 1951

TO : Commanding Officer
38th Infantry Regiment
APO 248

Section I: Administrative Checks

During the first half of May the Regiment was in reserve with the primary mission of training and administration. The Division Rear along with the Regimental Personnel Sections moved to Wonju, a distance of some 40 miles from the Regiment. This made it possible to send the 1st Sergeants, Company Clerks and Unit Administrators from the various companies back to the personnel sections to check and verify Morning Reports, promotion status of men, pay, Casualty Reports and various other administrative matters. A schedule was set up between S-1 and the personnel office for these personal to go back to make checks to insure that all units made this check and further to keep all units from going at one time. Under conditions like those in Korea and where the personnel sections are so far to the rear, it is recommended that the above mentioned system of checking be used whenever possible.

Section II: Awards and Decorations

A study was made during the month regarding the number of recommendations for awards that had been submitted by the Regiment and for which orders had been issued. This study revealed that 34 recommendations had been submitted as much as 3 months ago or longer, 55 for at least 2 months and 33 for at least 1 month. By further checking it was found that 30% of the persons that had been recommended were now casualties and were no longer with the Regiment It is recommended that recommendations for awards be handled more expeditiously and that orders be issued within at least 10 days after the recommendations are submitted enabling the unit to make the presentation while the action is still fresh in the minds of the men.

SECRET

Secret Headquarter report May '51

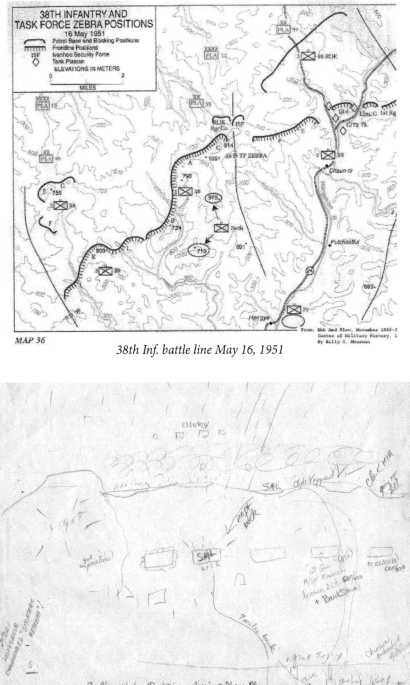

38th Inf. battle line May 16, 1951

Sketch of Sal's showing positions during May Massacre battle

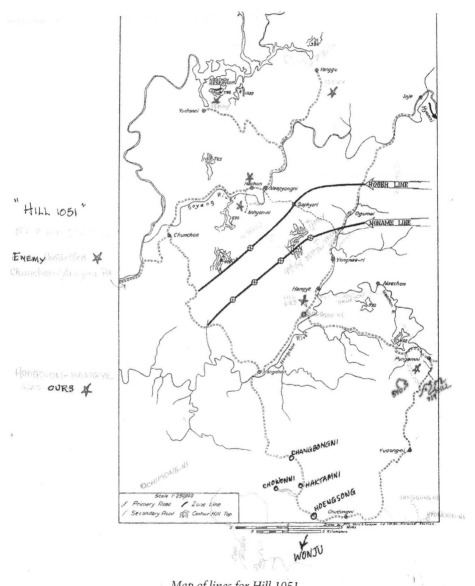

Map of lines for Hill 1051

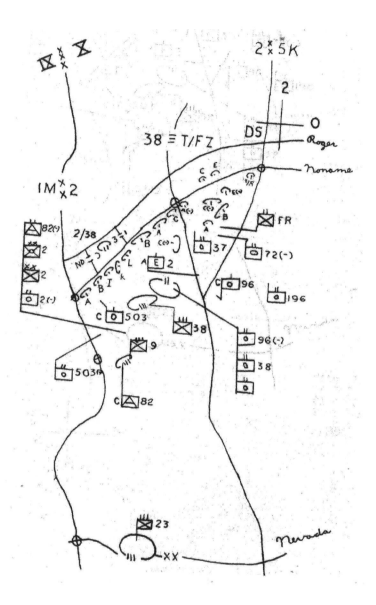

Closer details of 38th's positions for May '51

Firing at the enemy

Another moutain to climb

Second (Indian Head) Division

Distinguished Unit Citation

In the name of the President of the United States as public evidence of deserved honor and distinction the 2d Infantry Division is cited for extraordinary heroism and outstanding performance of duty in action against the armed enemy in the vicinity of Hongchon, Korea, during the period 16 to 22 May 1951.

Defending the critical sector of the Eighth Army battle front, the 2d Infantry Division and attached units faced a hostile force of 12 Chinese Communist divisions with an estimated strength of 120,000 troops. The Third Chinese Communist Army Group drove the full force of its savage assault against the 2d Infantry Division with the specific mission of annihilation of the unit. The right flank of the unit was completely exposed when enemy pressure broke through adjacent United Nations elements. Pressure increased and each night enemy forces by passed the staunch defenders and occupied positions to their rear areas. Tactical units of the 2d Infantry Division launched fierce counterattacks which destroyed enemy penetrations, successfully extricated themselves and through readjustment of positions stopped the onslaught of the Chinese Communist forces. Executing planned withdrawals and extending their flank eastward over extremely rugged, mountainous terrain, the 2d Infantry Division contained and held all enemy attempts to envelop and destroy the Eighth Army. The heroic and determined stand by the 2d Infantry Division and attached units provided critically required time for other Eighth Army units to regroup and block the attempted enemy envelopment. Without thought of defeat, this heroic unit demonstrated such gallantry, determination and esprit de corps in accomplishing this extremely difficult and hazardous mission as to set it apart and above other units participating in similar operations. Its sustained brilliance in battle, resolution and extraordinary heroism reflect unsurpassed credit on those courageous soldiers who participated and are in keeping with the finest traditions of the United States Army, the United Nations Forces and their own homelands.

Distinguished Unit Citation

CHAPTER 8

Rangers, Ridges, and Rescues

Only with your eyes shall you look,
and see the reward of the wicked.
~ Psalm 91:8 (NKJV)

The Airborne "Rangers" were assigned to the Second Division since February 1951. They found themselves "out front" just ahead of the 23rd and 38th Regiments. I liked these guys because they were "gung-ho." They were volunteers, and since I enlisted, I felt a strong bond to them. Often in a battle when I couldn't locate my men of "C" Company, I would attach myself to these guys. I usually found myself going on heavy patrol activity with them. They would go on long marches, singing at the top of their lungs, "You had a good home, but you left, you're right!"

They barked commands before dawn, they made a lot of noise crunching dirt with their boots going through villages. This part I didn't like because they drew so much attention to themselves. I tried then to quickly find my company.

In early February, the "Rangers" did night patrols also ahead of the Turkish Brigade. The patrols were dangerous but the most difficult was remembering the Turkish passwords!

According to "Ranger" testimony: when the "May Massacre" battle was beginning, and the 38th Infantry was under heavy attack, by dawn of May 17, the situation became critical. Completely surrounded with Chinese storming the crest of hill 1051, the First Ranger Company was attached by the afternoon of the 17 to the 38th. Later that evening, the "Rangers" were at the Command Post of the 38th, which was under increasingly heavy attack. By 22:30 on May 17, the First Battalion of the 38th Infantry Regiment Command Post was under attack and out of communications with the Regiment. The First Battalion was broken apart. In the first twenty-four hours of the Chinese attack, the Second Division artillery fired 30,149 rounds of ammo. Throughout the early daylight hours of May 18, long columns of Chinese forces were executing a double envelopment of the remnants of the First Battalion of the 38th and the First "Ranger" Company. This double envelopment was to break through a gap in the lines and then break apart again going left and right and then doubling back to surround and ambush our men. At 18:30 the First "Ranger" Company was designated as rear guard for the withdrawal of the First Battalion, in an attempt to infiltrate back to friendly lines. Going around a bend in the trail, they would come across several hundred Americans in the valley, milling around as leaders attempted to restore order to attempt a breakout. When daylight came, the "Rangers" could see Chinese walking around shooting fallen Americans. The American tents of the 38th Command Post were held by the Chinese, who were busy loading boxes of material and records into captured trucks. On May 19, "Rangers" infiltrated enemy lines and began to assemble with the 38th and together they succeeded in buying time for the UN forces to adjust and strike back.

"Winder" was a "Ranger" that I got to know later in the Korean War Association. He was captured but managed to evade the enemy for three months. It was his friend who got shot mistakenly, upon returning to American lines.

Right after the "May Massacre" and the beginning of June 1951, First Battalion of the 38th was given an offensive mission to command the peaks in the rugged hills forward of the Inje/Soyang bridgehead. The "Rangers" had gone ahead of us.

We were climbing very steep hills that seemed to go on forever. We seemed to be in the clouds. This first week of June 1951, I would mark my nineteenth birthday! "Walter" remembers this ordeal because he was walking behind a tank when the belt came loose from around its track and it snapped and whipped around his leg. There were a few minutes when the metal tightened so badly he thought his leg would be cut in two! He was evacuated with deep gashes in his leg. He was mended and sent back to fight again another day.

We stayed and held the area till we were relieved by a Marine Corps unit.

In the vicinity of Chungdong-ni, we had an enemy close-range encounter. The area was called the "Punchbowl" for it always seemed foggy. Our company was forced to withdraw to better defensive positions. That is when Sergeant "Nick" noticed his radio pack man wasn't with us, Corporal "Davis." We could hear him crying out. He was wounded and unable to reach the new positions. Sergeant "Nick" asked for a volunteer.

I answered, "How can I find him?"

"Nick" replied, "You'll have to follow his cries. We'll give you overhead protection, but keep to the right, don't veer left!"

Covered by a blanket of dense fog, I crawled out on my stomach, passing through barbed wire, back toward enemy positions. An enemy machine gunner was firing back towards my men, and it gave me the opportunity to locate "Davis." I found him in a crater depression that helped to keep the bullets off of him. This would keep us both from flying bullets over our heads! Laying low, I saw his leg was split open, so I put a bandage around it. I must have drawn attention because now the machine gunner was aiming fire at us, hitting dirt and everything around us! Trees were being splintered. I pulled my grenades and lobbed them toward the machine gun's direction. I heard the metal contact before exploding. My arm was on fire! I felt the shrapnel I got in the arm.

The machine gun was now silent. I had to quickly remove the shrapnel by myself, pulling it out from my arm. I couldn't crawl out otherwise and needed to hurry before another enemy could slide into gun position. I put the radio pack on top of "Davis" and, inching myself out on my back, I pulled "Davis" out, spread between my legs.

Psalm 56:13– "For you have rescued me from death; you have kept my feet from slipping, so now I can walk in your presence, O God, in your life-giving light."

When we got close to our lines and I could see the medics waiting, I called out, "Help me pull him! I can't do it anymore!"

They dragged "Davis" the rest of the way. We had gotten to a safe distance from the enemy fire. As I got up, I noticed that two of the men who were giving overhead protection were shot in the head, slumped sideways. Two other soldiers that were there turned to me and said, "You should get the Medal of Honor!" What an honor it was to be told that by other fighting men, and live to hear it!

"Nick" checked out my arm, and all that could be seen were splinters sticking out of my sleeves. "We'll have you checked after, because right now we need every man available!"

At least "Davis" was evacuated and not in enemy hands!

My arm became infected, and it wasn't until we would go into reserves at the end of the month of June (according to a letter written to us from "Nick" years later) that I would have a chance to have a medic check it out.

We heard that there would be a USO show, so we were eagerly anticipating having some entertainment that would relieve our war anxieties. It would be nice to have a little bit of home here in Korea! Marilyn Monroe and Jack Benny were scheduled to appear.

Deuteronomy 33:27 - "The eternal God is your refuge, and his everlasting arms are under you. He drives out the enemy before you; He cries out, Destroy them!"

We came back to a new rotation policy when we reached the reserve area at the end of June. This stripped the front line units of what was left of our most experienced men, many who mentored us through the war. Those of us that were left lost those who knew us best, and all that was shared on the battlefields between us. Of course, our loss was lessened by being happy for those who got to go back home, walking whole rather than wounded or dead.

Rumors of a cease fire at the 38th parallel had a double edged effect: there were men who were more cautious, or those who would take more risks.

No sooner did I enter the reserve area, I scouted out to see where my friends were. I found Lombardi from my basic training days, and who had been attached to another company unit. He filled me on some of our losses. After telling him I needed to get medical attention for my arm, we parted ways vowing to meet up after the war.

I wasn't expecting hell to get any hotter! First Lieutenant "Owen" joined our company's command. I heard he was a professional wrestler and that he played professional football as well. His first words to our men still rankle unbelievably.

"I'll bust any head in this outfit, and I'll show you who's boss. Anyone want to try me out?"

We had just earned the "Presidential Unit Citation" for bravery, and this was a mockery to the very reward of the seasoned soldier. Our tempers were like short fuses since our bodies were still wired from the last battles that had occurred just days before. Taunting the men this way would surely invite the fight he was looking for!

The men were stunned a new officer would address them in this manner. This was not basic raining, as some of the new replacements would find out soon enough. Perhaps we looked young like rookies, but a season of brutality had roughened us inside. Whether he was overprotective of his position, or felt he needed total control, this did not bode well for us. When no one challenged him, he searched out the biggest kid in the group.

Going over to him, Owen said, "You and me, let's tangle!"

"No sir," the kid replied.

Owen slugged him once and then hit him again. Still the kid didn't lift his hands. The rest of us cheered the kid on, "knock his lights out!"

When Owen saw that the kid was not going to be baited and defend himself, Owen shouted for all to hear, "if I see a coward, I'll kill him myself. I want to see everyone shaved and your grenades shine."

I thought to myself, did he think we liked having blood and grime all over our bodies, and dirt in our pants? We had stunk so bad the Company Command ordered water trucks out to our reserve areas every four to five weeks so we could wash and get new clothing. It felt like heaven to get clean, especially getting rid of lice that plagued us.

In Owen's defense, I have to say that his superiors at headquarters and stateside were enforcing discipline, not on our account, but because of new recruits and replacements to our units. It seemed that most of these new guys were drafted and none too happy to be thrown into a war. Still, corporal punishment was harsh since we had given so much of our lives already.

Sometime later I saw "Griego", but he looked different. It dawned on me then, he didn't have his handlebar moustache that he was so proud of. I guess it was shaved or get court martialed.

I wasn't spared the discipline either. My arm was infected and hurting where the shrapnel had gone in through the back of the arm, coming out shredded in front. It made a hole in the muscle of my biceps. I hoped they could get the splinters out and penicillin to help the infection. Headed to the medic's as Sergeant Nick told me to, standing in line outside the tent, I hear:

"All of you in line are court martialed! You were told to remain stationed at your company areas."

There was no reasoning with this man. Not only was my medical attention denied me, but my promotion to temporary sergeant was removed, and by that order I was to be reduced from Corporal to E-3. To emphasize his position as officer, Owen continued to punish any perceived infraction from then on with a court martial.

I believe my paralyzing seizures started to occur at this time. I remember laying on a rock listening to men moving around me. Someone was by the campfire, someone else was picking up a pack of cigarettes, but I couldn't move or say anything to them. I was so scared when the paralysis passed, I said nothing. I didn't mention it to anyone for fear Owen would punish me.

Isaiah 46:4 "I made you and I will care for you. I will carry you along and save you."

Reds Had Detailed Maps Of 2d's Position

By BILL BARNARD

WITH 2D DIV (AP)—A regimental commander who led his men out of an enemy trap said the Reds had detailed maps of 2d Division positions and had special orders to kill the wearers of the famed Indianhead shoulder patch.

Col. John G. Coughlin, Santa Fe, N. M., said "early Saturday we captured a Chinaman with a complete map overlay of the division position as of the time the Red attack started. The overlay was complete in every detail—those Chinamen had good intelligence.

"THIS PRISONER said the Chinese armies had special orders to destroy the 2d. They wanted revenge for the defeat we handed them at Chipyong and Wonju when we smashed their offensive last winter.

"They were directed to destroy our outfit regardless of cost in human lives. I must give them credit for a valiant effort but I must despise the commanders who sacrificed so many men on a hopeless task."

Colonel Coughlin led his fighters to a linkup with the rest of the division after three days and nights of fighting, much of it hand to hand. Enemy dead was counted in the thousands and Coughlin was confident the main Red assault had been thwarted...

THE COLONEL said his men had been warned by prisoners taken ten days ago that the enemy would seek out the 2d.

"If the unit on our east flank had not collapsed we would have piled so many Chinks on the minefields to our front that our own troops would not have been able to climb over the hills of bodies," Coughlin said.

"As it was they got around my regiment. We slaughtered so many their blood covers our boots because we had to walk over them to get into the new perimeter."

HIS OUTFIT was in trouble for more than 36 hours, the

"They poured into our lines despite our tremendous firepower. They cut off companies and battalions. But as we pulled into a tight perimeter our men still were anxious to fight. From one company a lieutenant brought in his men [as] they grabbed boxes of h[and] grenades as we broke them and rushed back into the...

"One battalion fought i[n] seven to eight miles over mountains but it rejoined [the] regiment intact as a figh[ting] force. Another had to slaug[hter] so many Chinks its b[...] were covered with the blo[od] of the fallen enemy it had [to] trudge through on its way [to] safety."

ROCK OF THE MARNE"   5 September 1951

COMMENDATION DELUXE RECIEVED BY 38TH

THE ROCK OF THE MARNE was driving north. Their objective was in sight but the going was expected to be rough.

Just as they were moving out for the final push orders came down to hold up – the objective had been altered because of heavy resistance expected.

But the 38th was on the move. A message went back to higher headquarters: "The dumb bastards can't take orders." The objective was taken, not in the two or three days they had expected, but in hours.

Probably the shortest but most eloquent letter of commendation to come out of the war was received from Brigadier General T. E. de Shazo, Second Division Commander.

Its complete text: "Well done you wonderful bastards."

PEACE TREATY CONFERENCE

Pfc. S[...]
Linwood St[...]

His platoon was under heavy mortar fire and was ordered to take cover. He dived into a bunker, only to find that it was occupied by the enemy and a machine gun. Sal lost no time in going somewhere else and was lucky to get only a few niches in the leg . . . Serving [...]

1ST BATTALION STAKES CLAIM

The mark of First Battalion has made its appearance further north.

The big sign "1ST OF THE ROCK OF THE MARNE" stakes out their claim to real estate around Hill 1179 and points north.

Miscellaneous news articles '51

DIVISION AWARDED COVETED CITATION

The 2d Infantry Division was notified yesterday that it has been awarded the Distinguish Unit Citation for its actions in the Battle of the Soyang River in which it turned back 96,000 attacking Communists during the Chinese Spring offensive.

The 2d Division becomes the fourth division to ever win this award. Those previously holding the citation are the 101st Airborne Division and the 4th Armored Division for action during World War II and the 24th Division for their stand in the early stages of the Korean conflict.

The award goes to all members of the 2d Division and attached units during the period 16-23 May 1951.

Upon receipt of the notification, Major General Clark L Ruffner, Commanding General, 2d Infantry Division, sent the following message to all units and attached units.

"I have been notified by higher headquarters that the Distinguished Unit Citation has been awarded by the President of the United States to the 2d Infantry Division and units attached during the period of 16 May to 23 May 1951.

"It is with mixed emotions of pride, joy and humility, that I transmit this historic message to you; pride in your great achievement in smashing the attack of 12 Communist divisions thrown against the 2d Division front and flanks; joy over the recognition given to your accomplishments by the award of the highest honor that can be bestowed upon your Division by our nation; humility in the memory of our gallant comrades who gave their lives for the United Nations cause.

"Members of the Division who have gone before us are proud of you and we place in the hands of posterity for safekeeping the Indian Head Division's motto, 'Second to None.' Signed Ruffner."

Newsletter about coveted citation

93

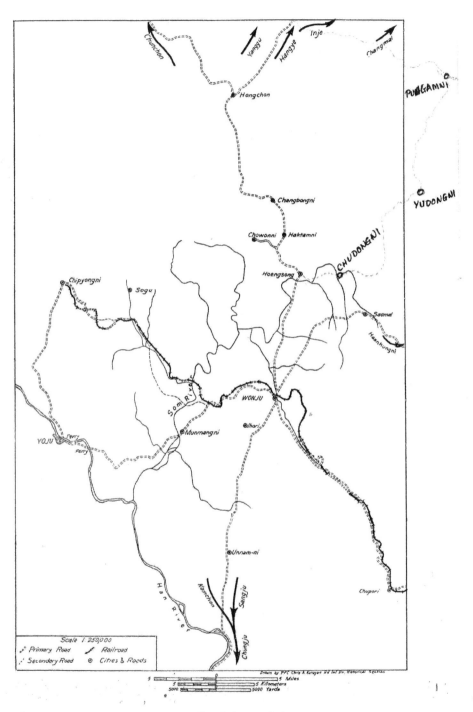

Map of battle lines July '51

Wounded transported by C-47 on litters to Japan

CHAPTER 9

Frantic Frenzy on
Fool's Mountain

Because you have made the Lord, who is my refuge,
even the Most High, your dwelling place.
~ PSALM 91:9 (NKJV)

With barely a week in reserves, by July 8 the Second Indianhead
Division received notice to prepare relief of the First Marine Division.

By July 15-17, we took over positions of the Korean Marine Corps
and the First Marine Regiment Patrols that went out across the entire
front to feel out the enemy. It was probably about this time, when we
were out on patrol in the mountains, that we came upon the body of
an American soldier. He was hanging upside down, tied to a tree by
his feet. A bayonet was stuck through his forehead between his eyes to
his chin. I cut him down and took his dog tags, putting one between
his teeth and giving the other to whoever was in charge. The soldier
had been a young, tall, lanky kid with black hair. He had a clean-cut
look.

Since we were on patrol, we had to leave his body until the body
bag patrol came to retrieve him. Dead enemy soldiers lying near-

by showed that there had been a skirmish. Clearly, he was left as a warning to us, the Indianhead Division. The enemy was determined to make us pay for previous actions! I wondered what happened to the Americans with him. His men wouldn't have left him like that had they had an opportunity. The enemy must have seen us coming and couldn't take the time or chance of taking their dead with them. This all had to have been recent because the bodies would have looked different otherwise, considering the heat. As frigid cold as the winter was, the summer was an inferno, with monsoon season around the corner.

Plans were drawn up to assault a hill mass called 1179, which the enemy had been using to observe the division movements. We were told that B-26's and artillery were coming to soften the hill before we jumped off.

Owen had a machine gun and was firing it till it jammed. He was on a berm-like terrain and I was below with another officer. He called to me, "Hey you, can you fix this? Do you know anything about machine guns?"

"I know how to shoot them, sir," I replied.

"You stupid idiot! I know how to shoot it too! It's jammed! Get here and see what you can do!"

After I spent several minutes trying to unjam it, Owen grabbed the gun back and passed it along to someone else.

"Hurry! Don't you see them coming?"

Owen had been firing for so long, but none of us knew at what. The enemy hadn't yet shown themselves. Everybody's nerves were frayed. Night was coming and we knew this was the perfect opportunity for the Chinese to infiltrate our barbed wire perimeter. Little is more terrifying than to be in a foxhole, listening and hearing unidentifiable sounds in the pitch black night. Nick went from hole to hole, warning everyone to be on alert as there was an enemy infiltrator slicing the throats of unsuspecting men.

Finally, the bombers came. They lit up the night. The sky looked and sounded like the Fourth of July at Luna Park! We hadn't slept for days, but we were now fully awake.

The attack was scheduled for July 26. The 38th Infantry was named attacking element. To us Americans this objective became known as "Fool's Mountain" and to the Koreans as "Taeu-san." Only a fool would attack this mountain because the terrain was so impenetrable.

At 16:15 hours, we moved out in a dense fog. All the weapons of the 38th Regiment, plus the Heavy Mortar Company of the 9th were lending us supporting fire. "C" Company led the assault with "A" and "B" Companies following. We inched forward, up the east ridge of Hill 1179. It must have been at this time that Owen's friend, officer "Hudson," got shot in the thigh. As they carried him away on a stretcher, I remember him giving us a hearty wave goodbye, and saying, "So long!"

His cheerful mood might have been due to thinking he had gotten the "million dollar" wound of getting hurt bad enough to get away from the fighting, but good enough not to be crippling. (According to the *Casualty Book of the Second Division,* Hudson was returned to duty the first week of September).

The enemy had been deeply entrenched in bunkers. We were getting picked off by their fire, despite the intense bombing of the B-26's earlier. Even the underground enemy factories creating ammunitions weren't affected by them!

The attack was on! Grenades were rolling down the face of the hill by the handfuls! The enemy grenades were round like baseballs. Some were sent down fast, or some slower, to explode at different intervals. Their fuses were about four seconds timing. Ours were seven seconds. I usually counted to three or four before lobbing my grenades so the enemy wouldn't have time to pick them up and throw them back at us! One of the enemy grenades rolled down at my feet. Thank God, it was a fast one that I was able to throw back! I felt like a baseball player picking up a fast ball and trying to strike out all the runners! We were continually running out of ammo so it helped to throw the enemy's grenades back at them.

Someone mentioned that there were plans for us in the First Battalion of the 38th to hold up for the night at "Cathedral Rock," a ragged mass of rock east of "1179." This was my battalion and resting the night within the rocks seemed more protective. At least the enemy wouldn't be able to burrow underneath us and go unnoticed.

As evening approached, Owen could be heard shouting, "Fix bayonets! Charge!"

I could feel the hairs on the back of my neck, stand up! Owen continued, "I'll shoot the first bastard that shoots!"

I had inherited the BAR from a soldier who went on R&R. "What about me, sir? I have a BAR!"

Owen charged away. No answer.

We didn't have long to wait for the enemy to attack in waves. I couldn't stand to see our men getting mowed down without a chance, so I opened fire with the BAR furiously into the enemy lines. Looking around, expecting Owen's wrath, I spotted him bayoneting and flipping one enemy soldier after another, over his shoulders, as though they weighed no more than a small sack of potatoes!

At some point during the battle, Owen called in an airstrike. Anticipating an order for us to withdraw to safer positions, I wondered why the order hadn't been given. I understood once I saw Owen, standing up on a ridge, shouting, "Come back, you yellow bastards!"

His arm was shot off, dangling by shreds of skin. He was bleeding profusely! Confusion and shock were taking over.

Isaiah 26:7 – "But for those who are righteous, the way is not steep and rough. You are a God who does what is right, and you smooth out the path ahead of them."

Everyone was running, scattering like field mice, our men and the enemy running side by side! Standing at some point on the red flag of the air panel, I noticed the jets were now making a pass. I could have reached up and touched the fuselage as he went right over me. I saw the face of the pilot! If only he could recognize that Americans were here too. At the speed these planes were flying they could hardly tell. Yellow rockets under the wings were released, letting loose a barrage of fire!

Second Lieutenant "Doucette" ordered, "Let's get out of here!"

All the planes came around again and started firing .50 caliber machine gun rounds. We ran. Bullets hit the ground on either side of my body!

Psalm 55:12-16 – "It is not an enemy who taunts me, I could bear that. It is not my foes who so arrogantly insult me, I could have hidden from them. Instead, it is you, my equal, my companion and close friend! But I will call on God, and the Lord will rescue me!"

Medics had reached Owen. I needed to find a secure spot. A rat hole was visible against the embankment. The planes were now turning, going higher in the sky and they were heading back. This time they were releasing napalm! Napalm is a compound of gelling agents mixed with fuel. As it explodes the liquid sticks to skin, or anything it hits, and burns!

Long, narrow bombs were falling, end over end, in the air. Huge billows of orange flames surrounded by enormous clouds of black smoke spread over the battlefield.

With no other option, I squeezed into the rat hole. I was very skinny but still had to wiggle my body in, only to come up against a dead Chinese soldier who stunk very bad! I pulled on him and then somehow shoved him out. By now I felt like the air had been sucked out of the hole. I couldn't breathe. Surely the planes were done. I needed to assess the situation before I suffocated.

Crawling and poking my head out of the hole, I could see napalm still splashing fuel and fire. The explosions were deafening! It almost camouflaged the sound of men screaming. Men were melting into nothing, burned to ashes. I felt I had surely gone to hell.

Quickly I inched out and as I got up, there were soldiers on fire running out of the cloud of smoke towards me! I ran, trying to pat the flames out on their backs. There were tons of bodies lying in the flames and smoky ground. My feet were burning! The soles of my boots were melting, it was so hot! I kept running. Earth, wind, and fire tried to capture me.

I managed to make it to a side of the mountain where there was less disaster. As I rounded a bend in the cliff, a group of soldiers came towards me. Recognizing they were Americans, I called out, "We need help!"

"We have to wait till the air strike is over," some Lieutenant answered.

Sergeant Nick and Walt were among the men. They had been scouting and got lost on the other side of the Rock, in the dense morning fog.

Most of my company was wiped out! We would have lost our colors if no man had survived! We had carried the standard of the "Rock of the Marne" since WWI. Secret reports received from Headquarters of the 38th Infantry state that 99 were KIA, 42 were wounded, and 12 were MIA!

Malachi 2:10 – "Are we not all children of the same Father? Are we not all created by the same God? Then why do we betray each other, violating the covenant of our ancestors?"

(The casualty toll of "C" Company, taken from the Casualty Book and morning reports show 30 wounded and 9 dead, a different number than Headquarters reported. This led me to investigate battle reports of 1951 compared to the Casualty Book and I found two full regular pages of casualties that had been omitted. I forwarded these to the Korean War Association for the 38th Infantry). Owen died of his wounds, Isaac was killed, and Griego was listed as missing in action, later declared dead. Griego was put in for the Medal of Honor, for his actions of repelling the enemy with machine gun fire while giving protection to his retreating men. Though he was seriously wounded in both legs, he told the men he would hold off the enemy for as long as he could. Master Sergeant Mattila was wounded, and as had happened to many of us, he was demoted due to court martials and would return stateside a private!)

As dawn of a new day broke, with the battered remains of the First Battalion of the 38th Infantry, plus support of other companies, a renewed attack would begin. It was already proving to be a hot day. We were sitting around, ready, waiting for orders when we heard, "Saddle up, and motor out!"

The young man next to me with stocky build and black hair mumbled, "I'm not going to make it today. I can feel it!"

I turned to him and said, "Don't talk like that!"

Jeremiah 4:19-21 – "My heart, my heart, I writhe in pain! My heart pounds within me! I cannot be still. For I have heard the blast of the enemy trumpets and the roar of their battle cries. Waves of destruction roll over the land, until it lies in complete desolation. Suddenly my tents are destroyed; in a moment my shelters are crushed. How long must I see the battle flags and hear the trumpets of war?"

Later, on the knoll below the hill, we got pinned down. For hours the enemy snipers had killed a lot of men. This young fellow with me got up, saying, "We're getting killed off. They will hold us here forever and pick us off till there are none left!"

He pulled a grenade and started running toward the enemy lines. His body was soon riddled with machine gun bullets. He managed to throw his grenades! By the fourth one, he was down on his knees, but still he lobbed it! He was enveloped in a white phosphorus smoke. I wasn't sure if it was his grenades or the enemy's fire that did that.

The Airborne Captain, possibly named "Taylor," who was in charge of our little group, took advantage of the opening in the enemy's line and ordered an attack. Shooting with all that we had, we pressed on. We confronted close to 100 enemy soldiers even though there were only eight or nine of us left!

At one point the captain radioed in and I heard him say, "I don't have enough men left to continue the objective."

I can still hear, "Court martial!"

The captain answered, "You can court martial me if you want but I won't sacrifice what few men I have left!"

Deuteronomy 28:7 – "The Lord will conquer your enemies when they attack you. They will attack you from one direction, but they will scatter from you in seven!"

As we made our way back to friendly lines, I found the burnt body of the young man who had told me he was going to die that day. On his chest was a burned Bible with charred pages fluttering in the evening breeze. A picture of a baby fell from the pages. We were instructed to keep personal items with the deceased. I left the Bible on his chest and inserted the baby picture back within its pages. As I lifted his body to put in a body bag, it fell apart. Maggots had already formed.

I can't help thinking about him and the image of the day forever haunts me. The worst is not knowing his name. When I try to bring this day back to memory, I want to say his name was "Robert." I'm sure it was self-preservation not to be on a personal name-calling basis. I can only blame my sadness for not taking the time to check for a name in his Bible. I do remember wanting to hold the Bible for the family, but someone said it would go home faster with the body. We would have all died that day, were it not for his selfless action and sacrifice.

John 15:13 – "There is no greater love than to lay down one's life for one's friends."

I never knew what happened to the Airborne Captain. I do know that we would have been all killed were it not for his compassion and courage. To have continued was suicidal! Waiting to get more help and pursue the objective was the wiser lifesaving alternative!

With a few more men gathered after the battle, we now were at a point where we had to move on and regroup with our unit. As we were running, I noticed the 57 recoilless on the ground. Walt later told me he lost his because he had been wounded and evacuated. I picked it up and ran with it while also carrying my BAR. Battle weary, it became too exhausting.

I shouted over to Lieutenant Doucette, "I can't carry the gun anymore!"

He yelled back, "Throw a grenade in the breach."

I did this, destroying the 57 so the enemy couldn't use it.

By the evening of July 29, the crest of Hill 1179 was reached and in possession of the Second Indianhead Division.

Taeu-san was taken with more than 115 tons of bombs, plus a total of 74,823 rounds of artillery, and 49,000 rounds of mortars. Tragically, the high cost of lives, too precious to count, is the most unbelievable to imagine!

Psalm 9:9 – "The Lord is a shelter for the oppressed, a refuge in times of trouble."

Two hills at Fool's Mountain

HEADQUARTERS 38TH INFANTRY
APO 248 c/o Postmaster
San Francisco, California

1 September 1951

SUBJECT: S-3 Evaluation for period 1 - 31 July 1951

TO: Commanding Officer
38th Infantry Regiment
APO 248

1. The training cycle started the previous month was climaxed by a training exercise for each battalion. The purpose of this was to demonstrate the effectiveness of the fire support available to the rifleman and to test the unit's technique of securing fire support. The exercise was conducted on terrain where a battalion had previously counter-attacked the real enemy during the May Chinese offensive. The exercise made new arrivals to the regiment aware of the firepower available to support them. These exercises disclosed a tendency to call for fire on barren slopes and to neglect the reverse slopes which the enemy occupies during our artillery preparations. Critiques emphasized this deficiency.

2. The relief of elements of the 1st Marine Division was difficult because of the smaller number of troops and weapons available in the 38th RCT in comparison to the marine units it relieved. The regiment was forced to modify the defensive positions in order to compensate for this shortage. Organization of these new positions was further handicapped by the numerous uncharted AP mines and booby traps in the area.

3. On 260600 July, 1951; the 38th Infantry was ordered to seize Hill 1179. The First Battalion was assigned the task. After two days the Third Battalion was passed through the First Battalion and two days later the hill was taken. Casualties suffered by the 38th were four hundred and thirty: 372 WIA, 46 KIA and 12 MIA. The enemy casualties suffered were: 124 KIA, with an estimated 1096 WIA. The enemies defenses on Hill 1179 were based on well built bunkers on the military crest of approaches to the hill. The initial artillery preparation was based on the transfer of firing data for entire battalions from single gun registrations. However, the sharp relief features of the terrain and the small target area made area fire on this type of emplacement ineffective.

Secret document July report dated Sept.'51 Pg.1

(Cont'd, Narrative Summary 1-31 July 51)

suffered four WIA and one KIA (an Artillery Forward Observer).[1]

Bad visibility held up previously planned air strikes but by 1400 hours fighters had arrived and were hitting targets as directed by TACP.

"C" Company, Netherlands Detachment and one platoon "B" Company, Netherlands Detachment crossed the line of departure at 260600. At 0710 hours, the platoon from "B" Company was in a blocking position vicinity DT180335.

"C" Company, Netherlands Detachment was split into two elements and by 260840 had taken positions on the forward slope of Hill 1100 (Objective 2).[2] At 0925 hours they engaged an unknown number of enemy at DT193346. They advanced to DT196344 and 190345 receiving fire along the way. Following a counter-attack at 1440 hours, the Netherlands Detachment withdrew under friendly air and artillery fire.

At 1430 "C" Company, 1st Battalion started a flanking maneuver vicinity DT207357 but were driven back before reaching the top of their objective.

All attacking elements were halted by this time by intense small arms and automatic weapons fire from an estimated two Battalions of enemy well deployed and well-dug-in. The enemy appeared determined to defend these positions at all costs.[3]

Meanwhile, 2nd and 3rd Battalions dispatched reconnaissance patrols to observe the action. They returned with no enemy contact.

By 261705 July, 1st Battalion, 38th RCT had succeeded in reaching the top of Hill 1100 but were driven back by intense enemy machine gun fire.

At 261740 July, "C" Company, 38th RCT was hit by friendly planes. All available helicopters and personnel in the area were alerted to remove the wounded.

1st Battalion withdrew under friendly air and artillery fire and closed into its original positions at 2145 hours. Friendly casualties for the period 26 - 27 July were 8 KIA and 99 WIA.[4]

On 27 July, 2nd Battalion dispatched one reconnaissance patrol to DT162318. Between 1440 and 1500 hours, the patrol received 6 rounds of mortar fire. They were ordered to withdraw and closed at 1520 hours.

1. C-2 POR #188 261500K July 51
2. C-2 POR #188 261500K July 51
3. B-2 PIR #150 271500 July 51
4. A-2 PDS #338 & 339 26 & 27 July 51

SECRET

Secret document July report dated Sept.'51 Pg.2

Carrying the wounded of 2nd Division '51

CHAPTER 10

Rigors, Rest, and Recuperation

No evil shall befall you, nor shall any plague
come near your dwelling.
~ Psalm 91:10 (NKJV)

The first days of August found the Second Indianhead Division adjusting its positions and preparing defenses along a line called "Kansas Line," a west-central area known as the "Iron Triangle." These were critical defenses, and would host the battles well known as "Punchbowl," "Bloody Ridge," and Heartbreak Ridge." Protection in this area was vital to the Seoul railway that brought supplies to and from the capital.

Morning reports list "Chappell" as a non-battle casualty on August 3. The rumor around camp was that he shot himself in the foot deliberately to avoid the battlefield. Master Sergeant Mattila and Walt were back on duty August 6 and 7, respectively. Both were wounded on Cathedral Rock.

"Booker" was rotated home. I remember him always saying, "I don't know why they took me. I gots eleven kids!" Whenever he was called upon to scout a hill, he would repeat this over again. One time he added, "I don't want to go up there!" Was he having an omen? I felt sorry for him, so I volunteered to take his place. Another thing I remember about him was that he drank his coffee so black, it looked like mud! His teeth looked bad, but he always had a ready smile and a very pleasant manner. Some pictures that I kept dating back to 1951 show Booker and Vaughn together with Sergeant Clark.

On August 14, Master Sergeant Matteo and a guy named "Smith" came back from R&R. Late in the afternoon of August 14, our division received orders to take Hills 983, 940, and 773. In support of the attack, the 38th Infantry had to also maintain one battalion on Hill 1179 and occupy two hills northeast of the ROK objectives, to lend fire support. We were to prevent enemy counterattacks or reinforcements. During this time there were more air sorties by fighter bombers and B-26's dropping bombs. We would have to walk again through napalmed areas. Gratefully, no bombs dropped on us. Just hot and smoky!

It was finally my turn to go on R&R to Camp McNeely in Japan for a few days, starting August 16, accompanied by a fellow soldier named "Gourley."

I felt like my inner compass was messed up. I couldn't find my way around. I don't remember much about this time, except getting lost in the city. This led me into some bad situations. In a back alley of Japan, another soldier, "McGee" came with me and we ran into some thugs who looked as big as Sumo wrestlers. They asked us if we wanted a good time with some gals. When we hesitated, they then demanded our money. I pretended to dig in my pockets, pushed at McGee and made to him do the same. When they let their guard down, we dashed out of there. We didn't care what direction we took, as long as we were running away from them. It paid to be young, skinny, and fast!

After this exhaustive and scary chase, I realized my arm was hurting bad. I checked into Osaka General Hospital where the American Military was examined. The medic was stunned that I had not gotten treatment already because my arm was severely gangrened. They had to cauterize the wound after cleaning it out as best they could, and my arm was put in a sling. I had a picture taken shortly afterwards, looking a little dopey, probably from the medication I was given. I remember there was a Geisha girl there next to the photographer. The picture shows how I might have been trying to smile to impress her.

I got lost again the day we had to take the plane back to Korea. I missed it by so little that I tried to run after it as it took off down the tarmac. Waving frantically for them to stop was useless. Someone told me there would be another plane in an hour, so I gave in.

When I got back to duty, I didn't recognize anyone. The 38th, supporting the ROKS, came under heavy enemy artillery and mortar fire. I didn't see Nick or any of my other fellows. There were some men attached to the 38th Infantry who looked familiar, so I asked if I could hang out with them. I obviously was not where I should have been because my battalion report officer marked me down as AWOL, away without leave, hours unknown. The little plane that flew me in within the hour had taken me almost to the front lines.

There was too much going on for me to question why I wasn't reported back. The survival of our men was at stake, and paperwork was never my strong point. I was focused on staying alive to accomplish my duty as a soldier, serving my country.

Psalm 144:1-2 "Praise the Lord, who is my rock. He trains my hands for war and gives my fingers skill for battle. He is my loving ally and my fortress, my tower of safety, my rescuer. He is my shield, and I take refuge in him. He makes the nations submit to me."

The higher ups decided and directed that in order to reduce the number of casualties during the cease-fire negotiations, offensive operations were to be undertaken only if they reduced casualties in the long run. I thought this idea gave the enemy time to breathe, regroup, and fortify. That is exactly what they did as they dug in deeper into the hills, and created "spider" holes, a defense of covered positions in which they could hide till we were nearby, and then they would jump out and attack.

I was back again with Sergeant Nick on a scouting mission when an enemy soldier stole our platoon scope. That scope, the only one in our company, gave us the coordinates needed for our positions. This tactical aid helped us to be where our economy of force could serve us against the enemy.

Nick turned to me and said, "Get him, Mac! We need that scope!"

I was the fastest runner in the group, so it made sense to me to immediately spring into action! I ran down the hill after the North Korean, grabbed him by the collar, and before he could knife me, I shot him with my revolver. I marched back up the hill and handed the scope back to Nick.

"Here's what you wanted, sir!"

There was no question of hesitating to kill the enemy. It was kill or be killed. One split second could make the difference between life or death. This was a duel to the death. Too bad world leaders couldn't fight it out among themselves rather than involving young men in the battlefield to die by the thousands. When you know in your heart that this is a person that could be your friend in another time but defense and survival of self and country are uppermost, sadly you see reality, and not murder.

The lesson was brought home to us later, when our group met up with an enemy squad. Coming towards us with their hands up in the air, they appeared to be giving up. They looked like a young bunch. I approached them carefully when someone grabbed me from behind.

"Watch out, they have hand grenades!"

Luckily for me they were shot before their tossed grenades could do damage. North Koreans and Chinese soldiers did not believe in being taken prisoner. It was considered dishonorable for them. To us it was a mind-boggling concept but considering their inhumane treatment of prisoners of war and even their own countrymen, they were possibly brainwashed into thinking we were inhumane as well. Also, they were influenced by the enhanced effects of opium. The only time I remember the enemy ever giving up willingly was the time we were in a town where the local bank was blown up. Korean money was lying all over the streets and rubble. Off to the side I could see some soldiers. I asked if anyone would come with me to check it out. No one was willing. As I slowly approached the group, one of them was holding what was to pass as a white flag. As they drew closer, I could see one of them being carried because his leg was so swollen from gangrene. It looked like elephantiasis! The others being carried and those carrying them were also suffering from various serious wounds and infections. Abandoned by their units, they must have taken a long time to decide to surrender. The realization that they were suffering a painful death if not treated, and finding out that we treated the wounded fairly, led them to come out. I motioned for them to come forward. I made myself sound the sternest I could so they knew I wasn't playing games with deceit.

"Ede wa." Come here was all I could remember in Korean.

I looked for anything suspicious. Even in this condition they could have something hiding in their dirty bandages. I escorted alone this group of about forty to our trucks. They would be taken to a prison area and given medical attention. "When you save one life, you save the world." (Jewish saying from the Talmud).

Isaiah 41:11-13 – "See, all your angry enemies lie there, confused, and humiliated. Anyone who opposes you will die and coming to nothing. You will look in vain for those who tried to conquer you. Those who attack you will come to nothing. For I hold you by your right hand, I, the Lord your God. And I say to you, 'Don't be afraid, I am here to help you.'"

On another day our platoon was halted by a sniper. When the shooting stopped, Nick looked around for a volunteer. Looking at me, he shouted, "We need to get him! He's out of ammo. We need to get him in order to move forward!"

"I'll go, sir!"

Gung-ho, yelling like a banshee, screaming, and running like the scarecrow Nick described, I jumped into the sniper's hole. He had his bayonet fixed but his look of stunned surprise was all it took to leap on him and get him first. Reflecting back on this event, I can only think: What if he wasn't alone out there? What if it was a trap? What if he was saving some of his ammo to shoot us at close range? Why didn't we just throw a grenade in his hole? We must have been low on ammo since I had to use my bayonet!

1 John 4:4 – "But you belong to God, my dear children. You have already won a victory over those people, because the Spirit who lives in you is greater than the spirit who lives in the world."

Monsoon season was in full swing, making roads and bridges impassable. We wore ponchos all the time regardless of rain or not. Ponchos and ammo were the only things prized above all we had. Even C-rations often got thrown away because it was added weight, except for the one can of pork and beans in the field jacket, like the one that saved Chief from a battle wound. We already had more than we could carry to climb, march, and fight. The hunger we had already experienced was nothing compared to the safety of ourselves and fellow soldiers.

Colonel "Mildren" gave the orders that the 38th Infantry would initiate the mission to seize Hill 1243. This hill was so high, I remember the crest looked enveloped by the clouds. We were then directed to move on to the west ridge of Hill 1181, towards Hill 868. We walked and marched so much! I'm sure the distance equaled going around the world several times!

Resupplying our goods and ammo became a problem because the hills were so steep. The men became pack mules. Each infantryman was made to carry three mortar rounds or a round of 75mm recoilless ammunition as he hiked for hours up the sheer heights even before reaching the line of departure.

(Signal to attack came at first light on August 31.)

First battalion of the 38th took the lead, moving up. It wasn't long before "C" Company became engaged in battle with two enemy companies. The fighting went on till dusk.

I remember a soldier, tall and lanky, I called "Frenchie." The French were attached to the 38th Infantry also. He was promoted to Lieutenant and earned a silver star. During an attack, I saw him pick up a machine gun, hold off the enemy, and give us needed cover. He fired back and forth for so long that he had to use a burlap bag to hold the burning gun! I shouted for him to come, but he shouted back.

"Keep going. I'll hold them off!"

I heard his shooting for a while, then nothing. I later learned that he was killed. (In the casualty reports on this day from our company, there was a "Godeaux" killed in action. He was from Louisiana.)

I'm pretty sure that soon after or during that attack, while running in battle, I found myself behind our 57 recoilless. In the split second that it took to register where I was, everything went into slow motion. I saw a soldier tap the shoulder of the one shooting the 57. I felt the back blast, falling backwards to the ground! I could feel gunpowder in my mouth and my face felt like jelly! Then nothing as I blacked out.

I don't know how long I was lying on the ground. I'm sure I looked dead. When I came to, all I could see was a blur. Faintly, above the buzzing in my ears, I heard someone ask me if I was okay. This might have been Walt since he told me years later that he had been using the 57.

I couldn't answer for all the humming going on in my head! The voice got louder, "Get up and run!"

Deuteronomy 32:3-4 – "I will proclaim the name of the Lord; how glorious is our God! He is the Rock; his deeds are perfect. Everything he does is just and fair. He is a faithful God who does no wrong; how just and upright he is!"

All infantry units broke contact and went into positions for the night.

Next morning, attackers moved out again. The battle would go on for three days. "Bloody Ridge" would leave us bone-tired!

Photo of Sal taken on R&R

CHAPTER 11

Encounters, Experiences, and Exhaustion

For He shall give His angels charge over you,
to keep you in all your ways.
~ Psalm 91:11 (NKJV)

Minutes seemed like hours and the days like one long nightmare. A living hell continued into September.

We were dirty, unshaven, and miserable. We climbed, were pushed back, and tried moving on again. We would fall, roll, and crawl up and down hills.

I clearly remember the following incident after we had just taken a hill. We were in squads with a leader named Sergeant "Payne" (although I later found out in the casualty book, this rank was a field commission, so he was still technically a corporal). He was husky, dark, and looked older than the rest of us. I thought he looked a little bit like Rock Hudson, in a rugged Texan kind of way. When I first met him, he was kicking a very old papa-san, a Korean grandfather carrying supplies on his A-frame. Payne knocked him down.

"Stop kicking him, Payne!"

As I helped the papa-san stand up, I heard Payne speak behind me. "You want some too?"

I ignored him and once the papa-san moved on, I walked away. We sometimes used the help of the South Koreans because they were accustomed to carrying large loads with their A-frames on this terrain. They were usually the older papa-sans since the younger men were fighting in the war. Women could be seen carrying large bundles in baskets on top of their heads, especially when having to evacuate.

Around this time, I came upon the body of a dead Chinese soldier with a small silver embossed box nearby. The inside was filled with white powder. Before I could admire the engraving, Payne snatched it out of my hands and flung the box far away, growling, "That's opium!" If I'd had the chance to clean out the contents, the pretty silver box was small enough to send home as a present for my mother. I didn't have time to get mad because we still had a lot of steep climbing before reaching the summit of the hill. As we made our way up, my legs cramped up bad. I stumbled. Payne came over, kicked me, and asked,

"What's wrong?"

"My legs are hurting bad."

He wanted me to show him where I hurt and as I did, he kicked me again harder in that area! I was so worn out physically from climbing, I had no fight in me. I was also still weak from the effects of the gangrene infection in my arm and the medications. I just lay there on the ground.

Payne walked away when he saw he couldn't provoke me. I was relieved because I would need to call on any reserves of strength from God for the battles ahead.

Hebrews 13:6 – "So we can say with confidence, the Lord is my Helper, I will have no fear. What can mere people do to me?"

Finally reaching a ridge, I had to take cover from the heavy enemy mortar and artillery fire directed at us. The enemy was positioned above on another ridge. I saw Payne jump into a foxhole. I leaped into another foxhole with someone else, about thirty feet away. A white phosphorus grenade landed in our hole and we were soon covered with smoke billowing out. The other soldier screamed,

"Let's get out of here!"

I didn't hesitate! We crawled out quickly, while burp guns erupted. As I looked for a safer place, I spotted Payne from the corner of my eye. At that very moment a mortar round landed in his hole. Payne took a direct hit and was blown up.

Rolls of money and film from his camera flew in the air, with photos falling everywhere. They floated down like a parade on New York's Fifth Avenue! His camera was scattered in pieces.

Proverbs 3:25-26 – "You need not be afraid of sudden disaster or the destruction that comes upon the wicked, for the Lord is your security. He will keep your foot from being caught in a trap."

Everyone had to regroup after that encounter with the enemy. Payne was killed (according to the casualty book, on September 2). "Fingerhut" and "Quinn" were wounded. Walt was wounded on September 4. "Winder," a ranger with our infantry, was captured with several others. After constantly being threatened with torture and slow death by the enemy, he managed to escape with two other Americans and evade the enemy for three months. Sadly, one of the men got shot by our own troops as they were reentering American lines. They looked so haggard he was mistaken for the enemy. Seasoned soldiers would have held their fire but new recruits on the verge of fear were dangerous.

While trying to occupy the ridgeline west of Hill 1181, we faced off with another enemy probe. One of our high-ranking officers got shot in the stomach. Having propped him up against a tree, Nick was shoving a wad of rags against the officer's wounds to keep everything in. As I approached, Nick spotted me and said, "Mac, did I hear you volunteer to evacuate this officer?"

"Yes, sir! Where to?"

"South!"

Nick didn't know I had no idea where we were, much less which direction was south! Any place away from this battlefield seemed to be a good choice. I helped the officer up, putting most of his weight on my shoulders. This took every ounce of energy I had. I noticed the officer tried not to lean too heavily on me. He must have sensed how exhausted I was and also figured out my dilemma as to what direction we had to take. He offered to guide me. We proceeded down the hill and I was thankful for the compassion of this officer and also the fact that we didn't have to climb.

This seemed like mission impossible, descending into a valley swarming with enemy troops and no backup protection except for us. We continued walking for a while till we came to a rushing stream. Our destination was cut off and it would take many unknown miles to by-pass this stream. I propped the officer against some rocks so that I could test the depth of the water. I waded in as far as the middle to check how high it rose on my body. Being almost six feet tall, the water reached my chin. The officer was taller than me so it should be okay for him. I asked him if he thought he wanted to try crossing here. He was weakening in strength, but nodded yes. While he held our rifles on his shoulders, I held him up. Shuffling along the bottom, I didn't want to lose my footing and cause him to stumble. In this fast-moving current we needed caution or we both wouldn't be able to help each other.

Isaiah 43: 2 – "When you go through deep waters, I will be with you. When you go through rivers of difficulty, you will not drown. When you walk through the fire of oppression, you will not be burned up; the flames will not consume you."

We made it across! Fully drenched, we barely crawled along but continued our journey. It wasn't until we entered a small clearing that we stopped. The scene before us was tragic. A couple of American tanks had been blown up and were still smoldering. I could see bodies hanging over the turrets. Once again, I set the officer down, making sure to camouflage him in some bushes. I scouted out the situation for survivors or any enemy lurking about.

I reported back to the officer that there were no survivors and no enemy presence. He agreed to move on. Resolved to renew our trek despite our weaknesses, we both knew he needed to get medical attention fast. Deep wounds could turn deadly in this environment.

Mental and physical exhaustion can play games on the senses. It seemed like many hours and many miles had gone by. We were walking in the dark, listening for any strange noises. Unexpectedly, we spotted an eerie little light in the distance, like a lightning bug in the night. Worry that this was an enemy camp made us extremely cautious. The officer wanted me to check it out first before approaching closer. We might need to backtrack quickly and avoid this spot.

Miraculously, as I neared the light, I recognized a lone MASH tent. It had become stranded in the middle of nowhere when the monsoon rains came. The rising water from the river isolated it from the rest of the division. Hurriedly and eagerly I went back to the officer to carry him safely the rest of the way. I hoped they could help him immediately because a long time had passed since he was shot.

Once we reached the tent, doctors' aides took the officer. Once my eyes got accustomed to the inside lighting, I could see they had been busy doing surgeries. I wasn't addressed or offered anything, so I turned to leave. Just then someone stopped me. They needed my name and serial number. I thought for sure I would be asked to sit or maybe offered some nourishment. I couldn't remember the last time I ate or drank anything. Feeling uncomfortable standing there, watching them try to work on the seriously wounded, I left the tent. Perhaps they only had medical supplies.

I ventured back into the darkness. I only had the very distant noise of battle to guide me back to my unit. I got myself scared thinking that no one would know if anything happened to me out here. Preoccupied with listening for sounds in the night, I retraced my steps, even re-crossing the stream again. My thoughts drifted back to the officer. I then realized, I forgot to get the officer's name! I had only addressed him as sir when we spoke.

Psalm 23:4 – "Even when I walk through the darkest valley, I will not be afraid, for You are close beside me. Your rod [to protect] and Your staff [to guide] protect and comfort me."

As I got closer to the battlefield and our lines, I started shouting to the soldiers positioned along the ridges. "Hey, it's me. Charlie Company, 38th Infantry! I'm from Brooklyn, New York. Don't shoot!"

I kept repeating this as I climbed the terrain. I thought the more words I could shout, the harder it would be for the Chinese to mimic. I also threw in the traditional passwords like Betty Grable, Harry James, Jack Benny, and any others I could remember the guys using.

Our unit had scaled the peak of Hill 1059 and launched a heavy assault on Hill 868. The hills were barren of vegetation from all the pounding of artillery fire. Trees were splintered and the ground looked like brown silt. Dirtiness was now our camouflage! We blended in well with our surroundings.

The battles raged on for days. Bloody Ridge cost the Americans 341 killed in action, and 2,032 wounded in action. This made it Korea's deadliest U.S. battle. According to the *Casualty Book of the Second Division*, the report for a week's time was 53 wounded, with 15 of those killed in action, for my "C" company of the 38th Infantry.

Hebrews 12:1 – Therefore, since we are surrounded by so huge crowd of witnesses to the life of faith, let us strip off every weight that slows us down, especially the sin that so easily trips us up, and let us run with endurance the race that God has set before us."

Barren hills after artillery '51

Medical record from aid station treating dysentery

Photo battalion on ridgeline for move out orders

CHAPTER 12

Pitiful Plights and Pestilence

In their hands, they [His angels] shall bear you up,
lest you dash your foot against a stone.
~ Psalm 91:12 (NKJV)

The war was still going strong. Our forces were going against a prevailing enemy, unmovable and secure on a very high and steep position. Being on such a pinnacle gave the enemy tremendous visibility. They zeroed in on any road or area we used.

Mortar rounds were pouring in while I tried running and shooting in the direction of the burp guns. These guns had a distinct rattle to them as they delivered ammo faster than our rifles. We sure wished we could have used those burp guns; however it was forbidden because mistaken identity would get you killed fast by our own troops if you looked like an enemy using their warm clothing or sounding like an enemy with their quick guns.

A mortar round came in, no more than twenty feet from me. I stared in horror as the boy in front of me was literally cut in half, his body severed near his waist! His cries of agony were heartbreaking. Then hauntingly he stared at me in disbelief while his life's blood poured out. Other soldiers were in pieces, not even enough to make one whole body. My heart continued to scream inside. My voice was silent.

Psalm 123:3 – "Have mercy on us, Lord, have mercy, for we have had our fill of contempt."

My attention was then drawn by a movement. A Sergeant, hit in the leg, tried to get up, stumbled, but fell back down. I turned back to help him, holding him up around the waist while he hung on to my shoulders. We made it to a safe place until he could be evacuated.

Psalm 138:7- "Though I am surrounded by trouble, you will protect me from the anger of my enemies. You reach out your hand, and the power of your right hand saves me."

I noticed that I was seriously bleeding from my bottom. My pants were soaked with blood. I showed this to someone. I believe it was Nick. He took one look and said, "Good God, get yourself checked!"

I was sent to an aid station which consisted of an outside makeshift medical facility. The wounded were in the open. There were no tents. I was put on the bare ground, stripped naked because my uniform was soaked with blood. A blanket was thrown over me as I started having chills, shaking uncontrollably with fever. The medics thought I was dying. They told me I was going home. That sounded okay until I heard the words "body bag"! I had lost control of bodily functions and was burning up with fever. I was diagnosed with an amoebic virus, commonly known then as "Korean hemorrhagic fever." This bleeding dysentery disease is now known as the "Hantavirus," appropriately named after the Korean river Han that carried all the germs from rodents. This virus infected thousands of soldiers during the Korean War, and most died.

Isaiah 40:29-31 – "He gives power to the weak and strength to the pow-erless. Even youths will become weak and tired, and young men will fall in exhaustion. But those who trust in the Lord will find new strength. They will soar high on wings like eagles. They will run and not grow weary. They will walk and not faint."

My wounded arm probably got contaminated when going through the stream while helping the wounded officer. It was still healing from the cauterization and was starting to scar over. I thought again of the officer with his wounds and hoped that he didn't suffer the effects of this virus. With quick antibiotics and care received at the MASH hospital, he hopefully avoided any infections.

For seven days I lay there. I lost 25 pounds despite trying to eat as much gruel as possible. I couldn't afford to lose any more weight from my haggard frame. I was eventually evacuated to a MASH unit on September 19 (researched from medical records at National Archives). Over the next few days, with proper medicines and a diet of oatmeal, I started to regain some strength and was able to keep food down. The bleeding slowly subsided.

Psalm 91:3 - "For He will rescue you from every trap and protect you from the deadly disease."

My morning reports showed I was reduced to private during this time. This had to have resulted when I missed my plane back in August returning to duty from R&R. A reduction in rank seemed so slight and insignificant compared to almost losing my life. I gave it no more thought and tried to stay positive.

At MASH, news was pouring in and the wounded were flooding the tents. I was hearing about the many battles taking place on Heartbreak Ridge. The word Heartbreak was used so often when hearing about the number of casualties that the name stuck. This ridge consisted of rugged hills, numbered 894, 931 and 851. They sat 1,300 yards and 2,100 yards apart on a north to south ridge line. The location was important because it protected the enemy's major supply route. Fortified bunkers guarded the key ridges from approach.

The enemy was directing fire constantly on the Red Cross evacuation trucks. Medics giving medical attention to any wounded, including even the enemy, were zeroed in on and shot dead. The red cross on the trucks and the special armband insignia worn by the medics did not deter the enemy!

The task looming ahead now fell to three infantry regiments of the Second Division: the 9th, the 23rd, and mine, the 38th. These regiments were now known as the combat teams, "Queen of the Battle." There were foreign battalions attached to each of the regiments now. Thailand, France, and the Netherlands, respectively. They were welcomed since our forces were quickly getting depleted.

I was reassigned to my company from MASH in a few days. I scrambled back into the trenches once again, facing thick bitter fighting. Sitting in a foxhole with three other soldiers, I was leaning against a board that was propped up against the wall of dirt. The hole was already splattered with blood and gory stuff. I tried not to dwell on this.

Mortar rounds were pouring in around us! One landed in our hole! I vaguely remember waking up on the side of a helicopter with someone strapping me into a basket. By early 1951 the bubble canopy helicopter would make the difference between life and death for scores of wounded soldiers.

"Where am I?"

I don't remember if anyone answered because I blacked out. I was transported to a South Korean hospital and treated for severe concussion, bleeding from the eyes, ears, nose, mouth. I was cleaned up and given a day's rest. I soon discovered I was the only survivor in the hole. The other three were dead.

My morning report states I returned to duty, back to the front lines on September 27. Only eight days had passed between going to MASH on September 19 for the bleeding virus, then being reassigned to duty, getting blasted by a mortar, rushed to a hospital, and again reassigned to duty! It felt like a hundred days. It should have been a hundred.

Psalm 38:12-16 "Meanwhile, my enemies lay traps to kill me. All day long they plan their treachery. But I am deaf to all their threats. I am silent before them as one who cannot speak. I choose to hear nothing, and I make no reply. For I am waiting for you, O Lord. You must answer for me, O Lord, My God. I prayed, 'Don't let my enemies gloat over me or rejoice at my downfall.'"

All combat units of the division were in contact with the enemy during the last day of September. On the first day of October there was a staff briefing by General Young. He wanted a plan to put an end to Heartbreak Ridge! His plan was to have all regiments attack simultaneously along with tank-infantry. This would keep the enemy engaged on different fronts, not being able to focus on any one particular area. Our tanks would spearhead the valleys, requiring less troops, while the regiments made the assaults on the hill.

This is the historical data from Second Division history book of the strategy: The target date for the offensive attack, October 5, 2100 hour, would require the 23rd infantry to secure Hill 931 and assist the 38th infantry in taking Hill 728 and objective "C," an unnumbered ridgeline which jutted south from Hill 851; the 38th, in the center of the division sector, was to assault objective "C" and Hill 485, a small hill south of Tut'ayon on the west. The 38th was also to provide infantry support to the 72nd Tank Battalion which was preparing to make an armored thrust into Mung Dung-ni.

Two days later, October 7, the 38th Infantry was given three new objectives – Hills 905, 974, and 841, plus a fourth hill, 605, situated 1,800 meters southwest of Mung Dung-ni.

On October 10, during the hours of darkness, the First Battalion of the 38th moved into an assembly area, in the vicinity of Kong-dong.

On October 11, fighting flared anew as the Second Battalion of the 38th struck out for Hill 905 from its positions on Hill 636, with the First Battalion following behind; that night "B" Company of the

38th secured the high ground between the two hills and "A" and "C" Companies pulled onto 905.

On October 12, the Division Commander directed the 38th to prepare to take Hill 1220. At 1300 hours, the First Battalion of the 38th moved out against light enemy resistance and in two hours had secured Hill 974, thus placing it in a position for its later attack on Hill 1220.

On October 15, at first light of dawn, the Third Battalion of the 38th passed through the blocking positions of the First Battalion and moved out to take Hill 1220. By mid-afternoon our objectives were secure. The 38th Infantry had succeeded in its missions! We were awarded another Presidential Unit Citation for our actions.

Isaiah 40:4-5 "Fill in the valleys, and level the mountains and hills. Straighten the curves and smooth out the rough places. Then the glory of the Lord will be revealed, and all peopled will see it together. The Lord has spoken!"

MORNING REPORT
RESTRICTED — 24 Sep '51

Co C 38th Inf 2d Inf Div — Inf

Wondang-ni North Korea APO 248 DT165262

NAME	SERIAL NUMBER	GRADE	MOS	CODE
Horan Richard C	03347	Pfc	4745	
Above 2 EM fr abs sk Hosp LTA Korea, to dy eff 13 Sep 51				
Walter A	3536	Cpl	4745	
Fr abs sk Hosp NRC Korea LD yes to dy eff 13 Sep 51				
Torndrae William J		Pfc	4745	
Villalobos Anthony J		Pv2	4745	
Above 2 EM fr dy to abs sk Hosp 5"A, Korea eff 13 Sep 51				
Jackson Jay L	655	Pfc	4745	
Fr dy to abs sk Hosp LTA Korea eff 13 Sep 51				
Taylor Thomas D	975	Pfc	4745	
Fr abs sk Hosp NRC Korea LD yes to dy eff 13 Sep 51				
Vega Victor F	987	Pv2	4745	
Fr abs sk Hosp LTA Korea to dy eff 13 Sep 51				
Cox Marshall L	731	Pfc	4745	
Carpola Richard		Pv2	4745	
Woolsey Lowell T	9	Pfc	4745	
Above 3 EM fr dy to LTA nr of Chajokchong North Korea eff 13 Sep 51				
Odom Sidney C	42	Sgt	1745	
Bake Oliver L	60330	Pfc	4745	
Above 2 EM fr abs sk Hosp LTA Korea to dy eff 15 Sep 51				
Donnelly John F	6731	Pv2	4745	
Fr dy to abs sk Hosp LTA Korea eff 15 Sep 51				
Stover Wayne T		Cpl	4745	
Fr abs sk Hosp LTA Korea to dy eff 17 Sep 51				
Duke			4745	
Fr abs sk Hosp Korea to Reld asgd & Evac to 155th Sta Hosp per A & D sheet 155th Sta Hosp eff 13 Sep 51				
Robertson Joe C	224	Pfc	4745	
Valdez Eliseo M	7990	Pv2	4745	

1

PAGE 3 OF 6 PAGES

U. S. COPY TAGO AGO GG ECO

MORNING REPORT
RESTRICTED — 24 Sep 51

Co C 38th Inf 2d Inf Div — Inf

Wondang-ni North Korea APO 248 DT165262

NAME	SERIAL NUMBER	GRADE	MOS	CODE
Above 2 EM fr abs sk Hosp LTA Korea to dy eff 18 Sep 51				
Rosario Jose C	36817	Pfc	4745	
Fr abs sk Hosp LTA Korea to dy eff 19 Sep 51				
Burcena Jose	51		4745	
Reduced to Pv2 per Order No 43 Co C 38th Inf eff 6 Sep 51				
Vanderplow Lester V	5		4745	
Reduced to Pv2 per par 1 Order No 46 Co C 38th Inf eff 15 Sep 51				
Vacaluso Salvatore	328237	Pfc	4745	
Nearchos Robert L	29134	Pfc	4745	
Smith Rheuben W	19316	Pfc	4745	
Above 3 EM Reduced to Pv2 per par 2 Order No 46 Co C 38th Inf eff 15 Sep 51				
19 EM Promoted to Cpl (E-4 Temp) per Order No 45 Co C 38th Inf eff 14 Sep 51 (Copy Atchd)				
10 EM Asgd & Jd fr 110th Repl Bn APO 301 per par 1 SO 167 Hq 110th Repl Bn APO 301 & par 4 SO 155 Hq 38th Inf Order 7 Sep 51 (Copy Atchd)				
Hemrick Robert C	82	Pv2	4745	
Race W Comp US TOS 2 yrs ETS Mar 53 EOD PEC May 52				
Hopkins Hollis C	3073764	Pv2	4745	
Race W Comp US TOS 2 yrs ETS Mar 53 EOD PEC May 52				
Above 2 EM Asgd & Jd fr 110th Repl Bn APO 301 per par 7 SO 167 Hq 110th Repl Bn APO 301 & par 3 SO 155 Hq 38th Inf Order 7 Sep 51				
Eastman Marlon T	8435	Pfc	4745	
Asgd & Jd fr Hq Co 38th Inf per par 27 SO 160 Hq 38th Inf Race W Comp RA TOS 3 yrs ETS Jan 54 EOD PEC Mar 52 EOD 22 Sep 51				
Hartman Fred L	033	Pfc	4745	
Fr dy to Reld asgd reasgd to Hq Co 1st				

1

PAGE 4 OF 6 PAGES

U. S. COPY TAGO AGO GG GU

Morning report showing demotion & evacuation to MASH

135

MORNING REPORT ... 2 Oct '51

Co G 38th Inf 2d Inf Div   Inf

Wondang-ni North Korea APO 248 DT165262

Macaluso Salvatore V RA 237 Pv2 4745
Fr abs sk Hosp LWA Korea to dy eff 27 Sep

Malchaski Johnny T US 7362 Pv2 4745
Fr abs sk Hosp LWA Korea to dy eff 29 Sep 51

Poole Jack L US 8600 Pv2 4745
Tagher John G US 94214 Pv2 4745
Above 2 EM fr dy to abs sk Hosp LWA Korea fr 29 Sep 51

Chapin Sanford A RA 59202 Pv2 4745
McCall Vincent E RA 98921 Pv2 4745
Above 2 EM fr dy to abs sk Hosp NB Korea 10 res eff 29 Sep 51

Terrell William R C 0931 1st Lt 1542
Fr dy to TDY Op McNeely Japan (Aprx 5 days) per LO 1-6 Hq 2d Inf Div (dtd 19 Jan 51) eff 30 Sep 51

Bal George R RA 123 Cpl 4745
Chun Ben S US 386 Cpl 4745
Slavaa Nicholas US 7265 Cpl 4745
Baran Richard C RA 3347 Pfc 4745
Above 4 EM fr dy to TDY Op McNeely Japan (Aprx 5 days) per LO 1-6 Hq 2d Inf Div (dtd 19 Jan 51) eff 30 Sep 51

Hobel Donald G US 0821 Pfc 4745
Tamarco Fowler D US 305 Pfc 4745
Bendove Egal B US 393 Pv2 4745
Above 3 EM fr dy to abs sk Hosp LWA Korea eff 30 Sep 51

Taylor Paul US 026 Cpl 4745
Fr dy to abs sk Hosp LWA Korea eff 28 Sep 51

Bowen Robert RA 57199 Pv2 4745
Fr abs sk Hosp LWA Korea to dy eff 30 Sep 51

Vorndron William J US 56588 Pfc 4745
Fr abs sk Hosp LWA Korea to dy eff 30 Sep 51

Motsko Harold V RA 5479 Cpl 4745

PAGE 2 OF 3 PAGES

W. D. COPY THRU NED OR DCU

MORNING REPORT ... 2 Oct '51

Co G 38th Inf 2d Inf Div   Inf

Wondang-ni North Korea APO 248 DT165262

Dowres Charles US56071337 Pv2 4745
Above 2 EM fr dy to TA vic of Wondang-ni North Korea eff 30 Sep 51

Ellison Walter RA08763350 Sfc 1745
Promoted to M/Sgt (E-7 Temp) per par 4 SO 152 Hq 2d Inf Div eff 22 Sep 51

Rudd Donald H 19 1st Lt 1542
Asgd & Jd fr Hq 2d Inf Div per par 5 SO 261 Hq 2d Inf Div & par 5 SO 116 Hq 38th Inf Cntrl Br Inf Race N (P) MOS 1542 Comd Gen Cat VII atg sect 50 D/R Feb 49 D/R 5223 Sep 27 Sec 50 Dty Plat Ldr MOS 1542 aero rtg on Spec Combat duty status

Promoted to Pfc (E-3 Temp) per Order No 49 Co G 38th Inf eff 24 Sep 51 (Copy Atchd)

PAGE 3 OF 3 PAGES

HEADQUARTERS SECOND INFANTRY DIVISION
OFFICE OF THE COMMANDING GENERAL

16 October 1951

SUBJECT: Commendation

TO: Commanding Officer
           38th Infantry Regiment
           2d Infantry Division
           APO 248

1. On 6 October 1951, the "Second to None" Division embarked on an all out offensive to seize deep objectives that had been designated by the Corps Commander. On 15 October the last and most important of these objectives was captured by the 38th Infantry.

2. The contribution of the "Rock of the Marne" Regiment to this all out offensive has been outstanding. You seized all objectives expeditiously and skillfully. The heroic deeds of many individuals were magnificent and your team work left nothing to be desired.

3. I desire to commend highly the 38th Infantry for these splendid achievements and ask that you pass on my congratulations and this commendation to all members of your magnificent fighting Regiment.

S/ ROBERT N. YOUNG
T/ ROBERT N. YOUNG
Major General, U. S. Army
Commanding

Commendation for 38th Inf. Oct.16,'51

Helicopter to MASH pg.1

Helicopter to MASH pg.2

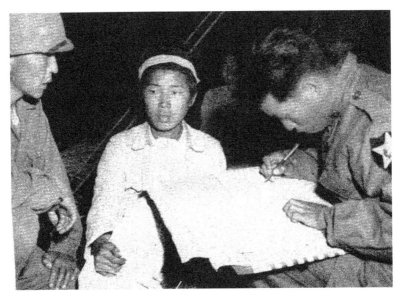

Photo of 2nd Indianhead Division soldier processing prisoner of war

Photo of helicopter evacuating to Navy ship hospital

CHAPTER 13

Sadness and Sacrifices on Heartbreak Ridge

You shall tread upon the lion and the cobra. The young lion and the serpent you shall trample underfoot.
~ PSALM 91:13 (NKJV)

(The physical and mental strength and ability over all the power that the enemy possesses and nothing shall in any way harm you, according to Luke 10:19)

The action on Heartbreak Ridge continued for many days during October as we tried constantly to get an enemy that could not be driven out of their bunkers. They had burrowed deep into the slopes.

Romans 16:20 – "The God of peace will soon crush Satan under your feet."

Changing my MOS from rifleman, I joined the flame throwers shortly after I returned to duty from the South Korean hospital. I was told it would be easier on me and not as physically demanding. My position would be far enough away from any enemy soldiers since the flame could reach at least 40 to 50 yards out. It was a relief not to think about hand-to-hand combat or jumping into foxholes.

(No one explained that the flame throwers were primary targets, picked off by enemy snipers! Flame throwers were never captured but killed immediately).

Called an M2-2, the flame thrower had a fuel capacity of 4 gallons and weighed approximately 70 pounds when full. The stream of liquid fire made from napalm gasoline fuel was propelled by a gas system of pressurized nitrogen. The petroleum was combined with acid and gelling agents just like the napalm bombs. The flow rate was controlled by a rear hand grip. The fuel was spark-lit as it left the nozzle and controlled by a front hand grip trigger.

We assaulted the enemy in their foxholes and bunkers. They retaliated by charging our positions full force, screaming madly like banshees.

I remember our companies often had to regroup and be joined by other units, because our numbers had gotten very low. Several times we were told only a handful of men survived in our company!

The "Eighth Army" fighting in Korea had many divisions, and many infantry regiments. One that I remember most notably by their patch was the "Hourglass Division," which was the 7th Infantry. They had been sent to Korea as replacements. Many of these soldiers were captured around the time I was, at the beginning of January, and were part of our group marching north, held captive by the North Koreans.

Another group from the Royal British Services were the "Black Guard" bagpipers. The story going around was that when they played the bagpipes along with the marching troops, the enemy ran out of fear. The echo among all the hills had to be astounding. Some said it sounded like the gates of hell had opened and the wailing was pouring out from within! The bagpipes were part of the defense platoon around the battalion Command Post, somewhere between the two forward companies on the frontlines and the two in reserves.

Our Second Indianhead Division was made up of 10,000 to 16,000 soldiers, comprised of three infantry regiments, the 9th, the 23rd, and mine, the 38th.

Each infantry regiment was made up of 3,000 to 5,000 soldiers, that was divided into three battalions with 300 to 1,000 soldiers, each. "First" Battalion had "A" Company, "B" Company, and "C", Charlie Company, which I belonged to, then "Second and Third" Battalions, with their respective Companies.

Each company was further broken down into three to five platoons or squads of 8 to 12 men, each. "A" Company was reinforced by a platoon like "Heavy Weapons,"which had the mortars and machine guns.

If a company had at least 50 soldiers and at the end of a battle was down to a handful, it meant that over 40 soldiers were wounded, missing, killed, or captured. If you multiply that, times all the companies of all the divisions, the result meant a lot of young men laid down their lives. Both allies and foe.

The men of the 23rd Infantry "L" Company had completely run out of ammunition and, using bayonets, stood their ground till the last man fell, including a Lieutenant Monfore.

Major units within the Second Indianhead Division were listed as following: 9th Inf. Regt.; 23rd Inf. Regt.; 38th Inf. Regt. (with attached French, Turkish, and Dutch volunteer forces); 15th , 37th, and 503rd Field Artillery Battalions; 82nd AAA Battalion; 72nd Tank Battalion; 2nd Engineer Battalion; 2nd Medical Battalion; 2nd Reconnaissance Company; 2nd Quartermaster Company; 2nd Signal Company; 702nd Ordnance Company; 2nd Military Police Company; 2nd Replacement Company; 2nd Division Headquarter & Headquarter Company & Headquarter Battery; 2nd Division Artillery; 2nd Counter Intelligence Corps Detachment.

Each and every one made up a military might to be reckoned with, not to be forgotten!

While out scouting between battles, I spotted a young girl walking in the hills by herself. When she saw my group of soldiers approaching, she started running and lost one of her shoes. I went down the hill to retrieve it for her. I hoped to make her stop. Holding up her shoe, I called out to her. Maybe because I separated from the larger group, she slowed and hesitated enough for me to approach her and return her shoe. She was all alone and looked like she hadn't eaten for days. She looked distraught and her face was gaunt. I asked if she wanted to eat, using my hands with the motion for eating. I next gestured for her to follow me. I remember when we got to camp, I found some food for her.

One of the officers in charge said they would take care of her and try to find her family. I spotted her in the distance for a few days. She appeared rested and her happiness at being safe showed her true beauty. I would have a wonderful image to keep with me, to endure the bitter fighting and the most vicious offensive actions the Second Division would ever undergo on Heartbreak Ridge.

We were to be substituted by the Seventh U.S. Division, who entrenched themselves in our old positions. The men wearing the "Indianhead" patch would be heading south for a much needed break after weeks of continuous combat.

Returning to the reserve area again, I immediately thought of the young girl. I hoped headquarters would have found her family, but selfishly prayed she hadn't left yet. I found the officer in charge and he gave me very sad news. She had been found raped and killed. They didn't know who did it. That her innocence and life were taken from her left me devastated. Deep down in my heart I regretted bringing her to camp. She might have had a slim chance of survival otherwise. I hated that there were men of such corrupt morals. The soldiers I was with were decent fellows. Some of the men I kept away from were men from the prison system. Our government offered reduced sentences, or cleared their records, if they volunteered to fight in the war. It would seem someone's criminal mind was among us.

Isaiah 27:1 – "In that day the Lord will take His terrible, swift sword and punish Leviathan, the swiftly moving serpent, the coiling writhing serpent. He will kill the dragon of the sea."

We were destroying the dragon, but could not save the maiden.

I received special orders that I would be going home. My soul already felt better knowing I would be away from this ungodly place. Already the first bites of winter were being experienced. While my company was in the vicinity of Sajokkol, North Korea, (per morning reports dated November 22, 1951), I was rotating out along with Baker and Gourley.

The communists agreed to resume the peace talks. I'm sure the devastating numbers of losses on their side was a contributing factor. Our perseverance would hopefully bring an end to this insanity!

I have my papers from Headquarters Camp Stoneman, California, showing we traveled aboard the USNS *Brewster*. I wired home from Sasebo and still have the original Western Union message dated November 24: "Coming home, Sal."

My final destination stateside was to be Camp Kilmer, New Jersey, but I would be first reunited with my family and friends after one year plus three days overseas!

Proverbs 4:25-27 – "Look straight ahead, and fix your eyes on what lies before you. Mark out a straight path for your feet; stay on the safe path. Don't get sidetracked; keep your feet from following evil."

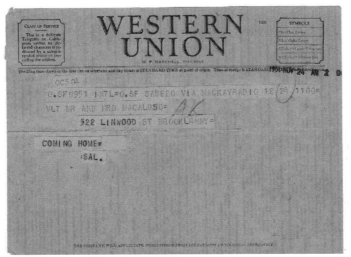

Western Union "Coming Home"

Helicopter bringing in winter supplies – winter '51

THE READER'S DIGEST ASSOCIATION, INC.
READER'S DIGEST ROAD
PLEASANTVILLE, NY 10570-7000

ELINOR ALLCOTT GRIFFITH
Correspondence Editor

Dear Friend:

    Thank you for your interest in Reader's Digest. We
have enclosed the material you requested.

                     Sincerely,

                     Elinor Griffith

This Correspondence Editor was kind enough to answer my request of finding any articles from the Korean War that may have appeared in their editions. Attached was the story written in the publication from Collier's, December 15, 1951.

Reader's Digest Correspondent Editor letter

The Heroic Story

Condensed from Collier's

Stan Carter

of Heartbreak Ridge

THE TIRED, unshaven major looked up at the chaplain. "They're taking a beating, Father," he said. "They're giving a beating, too, but not many men are left."

The major had just come down from Heartbreak Ridge, where American and French soldiers were fighting the longest and most costly hill battle of the Korean War.

These men thought their mission was suicide. Yet they crawled again and again up sheer mountainsides over the bodies of their dead comrades into the face of Communist fire. And in a battle that raged for 30 days and nights the 23rd Regiment of the U. S. Second Division wrested the ridge from a numerically superior enemy.

There were 1650 men, about half the unit's combat troops, killed or wounded. But they inflicted some 10,000 casualties on the North Koreans who tried to hold the bloody ridge.

"There's scarcely been a battle like it — ever," said Col. James Y. Adams, of Monterey, Calif., commander of the 23rd.

Unselfish heroism became commonplace. Pfc. Franklin D. Roton, of Sheridan, Wyo., had been a medic just three days. He was on the ridge tending a wounded man. A North Korean tossed a grenade. Roton threw himself over his patient to shield him from the blast and was wounded by grenade fragments.

Sgt. James E. Lunsford, of East Bernstadt, Ky., and Cpl. James Skaggs, of Columbus, Ohio, were killed going into a Communist bunker with nothing in their hands but knives.

Cpl. Manley Hand, of Sanford,

Collier's (December 15, '51), copyright 1951 by The Crowell-Collier Pub. Co., 640 Fifth Ave., New York 19, N. Y.

45

Reader's Digest story of Heartbreak Ridge

Mich., continued to fire his machine gun while North Koreans threw grenades into his foxhole. Three times Hand picked them up and threw them back at the enemy. The fourth grenade exploded and killed him while he was raising his arm to hurl it away.

During the first week of the battle every Allied attack was turned back by withering Communist fire. A wounded soldier at a forward aid station shuddered, and said, "It's a heartbreak, it's a heartbreak," and the name stuck.

The North Koreans had turned the four-mile-long ridge line into a fortress with 1000 log and dirt bunkers so sturdy that even direct artillery hits sometimes bounced off. The terrain was the most difficult in Korea. There were three major peaks on the ridge line — one at the south, one at the north and one in the center — with countless small ridges running off toward the valleys on the east and west. Picture it as the backbone of a fish.

Before the battle Heartbreak Ridge was covered with trees. At the end it was bald except for a few shell-splintered stumps.

It took two and a half hours to climb the center peak and up to ten hours to carry a wounded man down the steep trail.

Heartbreak Ridge was part of the main line of Communist resistance established during the Kaesong truce talks. It commanded the major Communist supply route. "We knew if we could get it, it would be a dagger pointing to their heart," said Major Gen. Robert N. Young, of Washington, D. C., commander of the Second Division.

But the 23rd Regiment encountered resistance stiffer than anything it had expected. North Koreans fired at them from bunkers up to eight feet thick, with baffle doors fixed so that grenades could not be thrown in. At times the Communist artillery fire was heavier than our own. It took three days of stiff, hand-to-hand fighting before a foothold on the ridge was secured.

The Second Battalion tried a dozen approaches to assault the center peak of Heartbreak Ridge, but came under deadly Communist fire and eventually had to give up the attempt. Direct fire from our tank guns destroyed most of the bunkers at the southern end of Heartbreak Ridge and a battalion of the Ninth Regiment was able to take the southernmost part with only four casualties. But in the next three days it lost 200 men while barely holding on. The First Battalion, attacking from there toward the center peak, was pushed back repeatedly by savage Communist counterattacks. The casualties were heavy. During one such attack two of our men, ammunition gone, were seen standing before their foxholes fist-fighting with Reds; another killed a North Korean with an entrenching tool.

Three days later the Third Battalion got to the top of the northernmost peak in a night attack with flame throwers. That night the

Reader's Digest story of Heartbreak Ridge pg 2

Communists counterattacked and by morning overran the American positions and killed everyone on the hill.

The First Battalion continued to attack the center peak from the south. On the fifth attempt 21 men crawled to the summit of the high mountain, but with the weapons they had they could not get the Communists out of their bunkers. Early on the morning of September 24 the Communists counterattacked. Few of the Americans got off the hill alive.

On September 29, Navy planes bombed, strafed and poured napalm on the center peak. Then the French battalion launched an all-out assault from the north while the First Battalion attacked from the south. The First was stopped in its tracks and the French suffered heavily. But six French soldiers crawled up the sheer northern slope of the mountain and spread a square of red cloth on the summit to indicate to Allied airmen that the ground was ours. Then they were killed by the Reds.

On October 5 the Americans and French again assaulted the center peak. At the same time a tank task force drove up the main valley east of Heartbreak Ridge, drawing the bulk of Communist artillery fire away from the ridge itself. The Ninth and 38th Regiments attacked from the west. At 6 a.m., October 6, the center peak was ours.

The North Koreans had been told to defend the ridge to the death and that was what they were doing.

They counterattacked violently. But the Americans and French threw them back and assaulted the last Communist-held peak at the north end. On October 12 Colonel Adams could at last announce jubilantly, "We've got it!"

"The Red defense was fanatical," Colonel Adams told me. "If they were my troops I'd be proud of them."

The medics went up to 72 hours without sleep to tend the wounded men, in the midst of small-arms and mortar fire. The First Battalion ran out of medical supplies twice because of the large number of wounded. The morphine and plasma were gone. The men gathered their individual first-aid kits into a stockpile and still they ran out of supplies.

There will never be a complete list of the heroes of Heartbreak Ridge. Colonel Adams said a hundred men deserved the Congressional Medal of Honor for their bravery. The names of many of them are unknown.

"There have never been American troops who have fought harder," said Colonel Adams. "The French were wonderful, too. Once they start, nothing can stop them."

There was a Puerto Rican boy who hobbled off the ridge on the stump of his leg after his foot had been shot away. He said no to an officer who wanted to call for a stretcher. Stretcher-bearers were needed more urgently on the top of the ridge where the really seriously wounded were, he said.

Reader's Digest story of Heartbreak Ridge pg 3

One boy — no one knows his name — was shot in the stomach five times, but he kept charging forward into the enemy until he fell over.

Pvt. Clifford R. High, of Manteca, Calif., reorganized his platoon after the lieutenant who led it was killed. He assumed command on his own initiative and led the platoon to the top of the last Communist-held hill.

Once during the action he was knocked unconscious by a grenade explosion and was reported dead. He regained consciousness and led the platoon on to its objective.

"But saying this fellow was a hero or that fellow was a hero — gee, it's hard," said Lt. Raymond Riddle, of Dearborn, Mich. "You see, there were so many."

Reader's Digest story of Heartbreak Ridge pg 3 continued

Photo of battlefield positions on ridge '51

Holding the line

Peace talk lunch break

Treating the wounded children

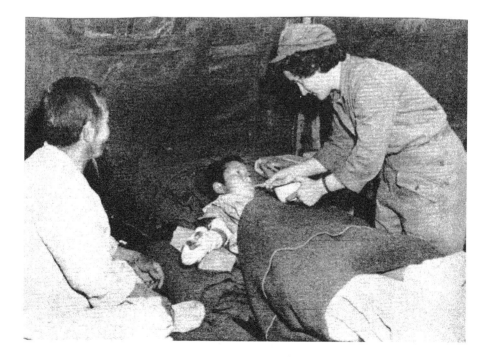

Wounded young enemy soldier

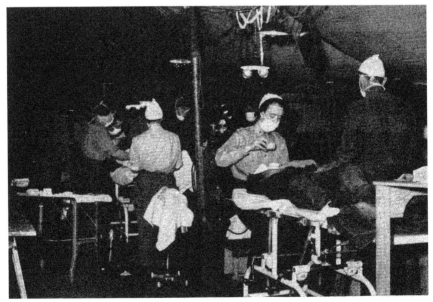

MASH

*Indomitable spirit
of orphans in Korea*

*Orphanage of boys
at 38th parallel*

Korean boy at play

Notre Dame star with Korean orphan boy

Village girls in Korea '51

Korean village children

Help for orphanage in Pohang by Marine Air Wing

CHAPTER 14

Recollections, Regrets, and Righteousness

Because he has set his love upon Me, therefore will I deliver him;
I will set him on high, because he has known My name.
~ PSALM 91:14 (NKJV)

I remember many names of the soldiers in my unit because they touched my life, from basic training to the beginning of my tour of duty in Korea, or because of photos that I preserved since the war. Regretfully those who came after the first major battles were difficult to remember or lost to memory. It wasn't that I didn't want to know anyone by name, but I believe it was a mental dissociation from having one more to mourn. Never forgotten in my heart.

Matthew 5:4 – "God blesses those that mourn, for they will be comforted."

Sergeant "Penny" was an older soldier, probably in his thirties. He sported a big, long handlebar mustache. He got shot through the ankle while I was standing next to him. After tying off his wound, I helped him shuffle down the road, hugging the side of the hill to avoid incoming enemy fire. Later he would be evacuated.

Corporal "Vaughn" was a small guy, with light brown hair. He came from Tennessee. He lost a chunk of his arm but was able to return to duty, fighting alongside us again. Vaughn would "call in" to the tanks any enemy locations, aim direction, or any adjustments to the line of fire.

It was while he and I were walking over a small hill that two tanks, some distance behind our men, were prepared to shoot, giving us cover. Usually, we walked behind the tanks but on this particular day they didn't want to give away their positions. We were told of a large enemy presence in this vicinity, and surprise was a key to success in any battle.

I spotted about two hundred enemy soldiers dug in on the side of the hill. I was so energized by adrenaline that I forgot to have Vaughn put the call in, and ran back down to the tanks shouting, "They're there! Shoot, shoot!"

I always seemed to be running, which is why I earned the nickname, "Scarecrow." I could hear a muffled reply from within the tank.

"Wait till some reach the top of the hill!"

It didn't take long for the first round of enemy to appear. I noticed that they formed lines of attack in columns. This helped in the event the soldier in front got hit, the next guy behind picked up the first soldier's weapon. This procession lasted till the last soldier, looking like waves of bodies.

The tops of their heads were now visible. The tankers let loose a barrage of gunfire and blew away the hilltop, along with dozens of the enemy soldiers.

Sergeant "Hammer," a short, blond, stocky fellow, would lead our patrol giving the point signs. We were constantly on the lookout. I had the BAR at the time, inherited from "Big Soldier" who was on R&R. When Hammer gave the signal designating an enemy machine gunner on a hill, I fired and did away with as much of the threat as possible. It was that kind of teamwork that kept us alive. Everyone did their part for survival.

One of our platoon leaders was Sergeant "Foley." He was older than the rest of us, short and good looking. His assistant was "Quinn," a Jersey boy that had made it to Sergeant First Class. I got to know Quinn better when we returned home, back in Fort Dix, New Jersey. We found ourselves together in the stockade at Ft. Dix. During his time overseas, he had been demoted too. Our battle records were either lost or did not get filed till months later and he had to testify on my behalf that I was present in Korea. I was grateful he had been in my unit and knew me better than most. No one could tell what I had gone through just by looking at me. Quinn's legs were badly stitched up. I don't know how he walked without bleeding from his wounds. I was one of the walking wounded. My head was killing me but no one listened.

"Bell," who had gotten the BAR from "Big Soldier" when he rotated home, in turn gave it to me when he rotated home. Bell gave haircuts with sheep shears, and I believe he may have been the one to butcher the abandoned cow early in the war. He was a Native American Indian, as well as "Fingerhut," who was from Wisconsin. We also had our Company Major, "Chief," from the Maidu Indian tribe in California.

"Gordon" was my ammo bearer for the BAR. He had red hair and freckles. This reminds me of "Maybin," who was my friend from basic training. The men nicknamed Maybin "Red" because he had dark red hair. He was evacuated after the May Massacre battle and by December was sent to Hawaii.

Sergeant "Banks" was friends with "Two-Gun Mairich." Banks was pock faced and stood about 5'9". He survived being wounded three times, lastly in the May Massacre. Quite often the two friends would play cards when in reserves. Most of the betting or gambling was done for better provisions. If someone found a can of beer, it was worth a fortune. Homemade cookies from home, if they survived reaching us out in the field, were priceless! I didn't drink beer, so I always made sure to trade for better goodies.

Mairich died of his wounds in captivity. Both Mairich and McCracken were listed in casualty reports as "died while in captivity." Neither was mentioned as WIA (wounded in action). Moose and Captain White were mentioned as RMC (returned to military control), not POW. These two men spent two years in an enemy prison camp and weren't released until August 1953. This would seem to conflict with records.

The company chaplain, though I can't remember his name, played an important part in our lives. From the very beginning he would visit us in our foxholes, especially when we were anticipating an enemy attack. He always reminded us of God presence and prayed with us, chasing our fears away.

"God is with you. Be blessed and stay safe!"

Men always came when the chaplain held services. We were in the devil's paradise, a chaotic world of utter disorder, destruction, and misrule. Truly a living hell! Often soldiers became a law unto themselves. We needed to bring God back into our lives.

What would haunt me is what a nun screamed at me back in school. "You'll die with your boots on!" This was the title of an early Errol Flynn movie, but the memory of it still upset me.

Exemplary actions of men alongside me in Korea are two Medal of Honor recipients, "Father Emil Kapaun" and "Ted," a Jewish soldier. They were not in my company, but they were above all, second to none!

Father Kapaun, an Army chaplain, calmly walked through withering enemy fire. It was described by fellow soldiers that he used hand-to-hand combat to provide assistance to soldiers. He didn't fire a gun. He comforted, provided medical aid, and he carried the wounded to safety when he could. Love for his fellow brothers was the mightiest weapon and he was willing to die for them. Taken prisoner, he offered his clothes during the freezing winter, sneaked out to bring back grain, and tended the wounded in the camps. Guards tortured him for his show of faith and compassion, putting him in isolation, beaten and sick, without food or water. (He died and his remains were finally returned home in 2021.) Those that survived the prison camp testified that he saved many of them, including those he saved in combat.

Father Emil Kapaun was honored with the Medal of Honor in April 2013.

Ted was a Hungarian-born Holocaust survivor. At the age of fifteen, in 1948, he immigrated to the United States. By 1950, at the age of 18, Ted joined the U.S. Army and found himself serving in the war in Korea. He was consistently volunteered for the most dangerous patrols and missions. During one mission in October 1950, he was ordered to secure a hill, giving his rifle company a badly and timely needed route of retreat. Single-handedly he managed to defend the hill for 24 hours by placing explosives and ammunition strategically. The enemy soldiers assumed they were fighting a large number of our troops. Ted was severely wounded during this time, captured, and spent 30 months in a prison camp. Faced with constant hunger, filth, and disease, his spirit of "never give up" helped his fellow men. I can't imagine going through two extreme prison camp experiences in a lifetime!

Hebrews 11:1 - "Faith is the confidence that what we hope for will actually happen; it gives us assurance about things we cannot see."

Almost every evening Ted would escape from the prison camp and steal food from the enemy storehouses and gardens, only to sneak back into camp to provide desperately needed care and moral support for the sick and wounded. His efforts attributed to saving the lives of at least 40 fellow prisoners who testified on his behalf.

Ted was awarded the Medal of Honor in 2005 for his Korean War feats.

There were 8 Medal of Honor recipients from the Second Indianhead Division, and there were 12 whose decorations were pending by the end of the war.

The units listed below account for 96% of the Americans killed by hostile action in Korea. Wounded in action include only those actually hospitalized.

Major U.S. Combat Unit

CASUALTIES IN KOREA

UNIT	KILLED IN ACTION	WOUNDED IN ACTION
2nd Infantry Division	7,094	16,575
1st Marine Division	4,004	25,864
7th Infantry Division	3,905	10,858
1st Cavalry Division	3,811	12,086
24th Infantry Division	3,735	7,395
25th Infantry Division	3,048	10,188
3rd Infantry Division	2,160	7,939
Far East Air Force/5th Air Force	1,200	368
5th Regimental Combat Team	867	3,188
45th Infantry Division	834	3,170
Naval Forces Far East/7th Fleet	458	1,576
187th Airborne Regimental Combat Team	447	1,656
40th Infantry Division	376	1,457
1st Marine Aircraft Wing	258	174

29th RCT was attached to the 24th ID and later assigned to the 27th and 35th Inf. Regts. of the 25th ID. It lost 313 men KIA on July 25-26, 1950. Those figures are included above.

In addition to the units listed, 1,432 Army personnel assigned to outfits independent of the divisions and RCTs were also KIA.

SOURCE: Battle Casualties of the Army, 30 September 1954 (Office Assistant Chief of Staff, G-1, Dept. of the Army) and other sources.

Insignias of Divisions fighting in Korean War

Hamer

Basic Training 1950
Lovering & McCracken

Maybin & Sal

Hamer

April 1951

Sal

Hoppy

Sal

Sal and men of 38th Inf. Apr.'51

Hogan and Welch Apr.'51

SITTING:
CHAPPEL, 1st;
WALTER, in
middle, w/
helmet.

L→R
BOOKER,
VAUGHN,
CLARK

BAKER
SITTING

BAKER
ON
RIGHT

Baker and Company C men '51

CHAPTER 15

Home, Health, and Hell

He shall call upon Me, and I will answer him; I will be
with him in trouble;I will deliver him and honor him.
~ PSALM 91:15 (NKJV)

I finally was going home to my family, after being gone one year and three days. My time spent overseas was listed on my DD-214, as well as my Combat Infantry Badge awarded February 2, 1951. Frontline combat started January 2, 1951. It felt like years had gone by.

My wounds were just scabs now. The shrapnel in my head was still there but invisible. Aside from splitting headaches, I wasn't made aware of any damages in my head till much later. Soon my aches and pains came tenfold, accompanied by chills and fevers.

I had only four teeth left in my mouth. The others were knocked out from the concussions and the penetrating head wound. The Army promised me dentures stateside. It took more than a dozen years for them to be delivered to me. They went from California, where I was stationed, to New York, where I lived, and finally Florida, where I moved for my health! Imagine my surprise in finding they were made of metal! Once in my mouth, I looked like the big, bad guy in the

James Bond movie, nicknamed "Jaws." Food tasted awful. There was no way I could use them! It would be a while before I found a dentist who would help financially. He got paid, but he also treated me on the condition that I give him the interesting platinum dentures. I was so happy to be rid of them and to be able to eat properly again. I needed to gain back the weight I had lost from not eating properly.

The hair on my legs was permanently gone from frostbite that first winter in Korea. My toes still tingled and were numb when I wore my shoes. My civilian footwear of choice turned out to be loafers, even though my skinny ankles and feet looked like I was wearing boats! If my Army buddies could have seen me, I would have been given many more nicknames. No complaining here because too many friends went home without legs or arms—or not at all.

I remember nothing about sailing home or my arrival back to the United States. A fellow soldier who was on the same ship coming home with me sent copies of our shipping orders. The Western Union message, "Coming home," indicated the date of my departure from overseas. My mother had saved it, along with the many letters I wrote home. During one of my painful flashbacks I made the mistake of burning some of the letters. Another time I threw away what was left of the letters. I wanted no reminders. (Sadly, these might have contained more information about people and places).

I remember my homecoming as a big letdown. Everyone was carrying on with their lives, not realizing a terrible war was raging in Korea. I would try to talk about the horrendous struggles of our soldiers over there and what the war was like. Quickly I was hushed up. "Forget about it."

When I spoke about my experiences, I was met with skepticism and unbelief. I felt isolated and started to withdraw from my family and friends. The bond I had with my fellow combat soldiers was gone and now I was alone. No one believed me or cared what I had gone through! Friends and neighbors would greet me and say, "Hi, where have you been?"

Psalm 102:2 – "Don't turn away from me in my time of distress. Bend down to listen, and answer me quickly when I call to you."

I wasn't expecting a parade upon my return, but I didn't think so little would be thought of the sacrifices our Army and military buddies experienced. Communism was trying to take a foothold in another allied country and no one seemed to care.

The daily news reported deaths of soldiers I knew. I developed an overwhelming sense of guilt for surviving. It was plaguing me. My graduation roster from Fort Knox was dotted black all over from ink marks alongside the pictures of the deceased boys.

It would later be written in a book, *This Kind of War* by T. R. Fehrenbach, that "the Second Division inflicted more casualties during the Korean War than any other, but always had the misfortune of losing 50% more men than other divisions."

The Second Indianhead Division participated in all ten of the named campaigns of the war. The casualties were 7,094 men killed and 16,575 wounded in action (per the VFW magazine issue June 1988); M.I.A. were still to be accounted for.

I was in 4 Korean War Campaigns from the beginning of January 1951 to the end of November 1951. The Korean War Campaigns were as follows:

UN Defensive	June 27- Sept. 15, 1950
UN Offensive	Sept. 16 – Nov. 2, 1950
CCF (Chinese) Intervention	Nov. 3, 1950 – Jan. 24, 1951
First UN Counter Offensive	Jan.25 – April 21, 1951
CCF (Chinese) Spring Offensive	April 22 – July 8, 1951
UN Summer-Fall Offensive	July 9 – Nov.27, 1951
Second Korean Winter	Nov.28, 1951 – April 30, 1952
Korea, Summer-Fall 1952	May 1, - Nov. 30, 1952
Third Korean Winter	Dec. 1, 1952 – April 30, 1953
Korea, Summer 1953	May 1 – July 27, 1953

Because I would be listed as an eyewitness on the rosters, many family members of the killed in action tried contacting me to ask about their loved ones.

"How did he die?"

A priest came to my house on behalf of the soldier who sang "The Old Rugged Cross." His fiancée wanted to know about his last days, what he said, whether he mentioned her, and how he died. After trying to recall all that I could to the priest, I locked myself in my parents' basement.

It was a crazy time. Flashbacks were extremely painful. Grief would overtake me again. I tried burying my sorrows in a bottle. I tried to hide going crazy from family and friends. I felt like the demons of hell were after me! Fits of mental anguish had the Army doctors temporarily putting me in a mental institution. In there, one could become even crazier, from electric shock treatments to being sprayed with a fire hose.

"On a hill far away, stood an old, rugged Cross, the emblem of suffering and shame …"

Psalm 102:3-5 "For my days disappear like smoke, and my bones burn like red-hot coals. My heart is sick, withered like grass, and I have lost my appetite. Because of my groaning, I am reduced to skin and bones."

It was too painful to remember. My mother must have put a stop to any Army contacts, because I heard from no one else after the priest left. Some of my buddies tried to find me after the war, but she turned them away. I can't blame her since she saw firsthand the results of war and the nightmares. My head felt like it was in a vise grip with splitting headaches. My fevers and chills caused me to be bedridden. My hands shook, even under layers of blankets. I felt like my guts were being torn up inside and I even coughed up blood.

Maybe if I had talked with some of my combat buddies, it would have helped to share and unload the burdens and griefs. I tried the

Veterans Administration but they were not equipped to deal with severe post-trauma. My military service paperwork was messed up and didn't support the medical attention I needed. They called me anxious, and gladly would have put me in an asylum were it not for the persistence of my parents. So many soldiers after the war were put in mental institutions because their families or friends didn't know how to help them, or there was no one to turn to.

I couldn't walk along the streets of Brooklyn because of all the city noise and the backfire of vehicles. It was embarrassing to take a girl out on a date and end up taking cover in a ditch. I had been going out with a girl before the war but I don't remember writing her or receiving any letters from her. She officially broke up with me after my return. Considering what a nervous wreck I became, who could blame her? I would be leaving again soon since I was still in the service so it was best that it ended.

This reminds me of a Britcom, *As Time Goes By*. A young English soldier who was going to fight in Korea fell in love with a nurse played by Judi Dench. When he leaves, she writes to him and he writes to her, but neither letter reaches them. Each thinks the other is no longer interested. She marries someone else and he goes to Kenya after the war to run a coffee plantation. They meet 38 years later. She's widowed and he's divorced, allowing them to pick up where they left off, to love and marry, happily ever after, as the TV show portrayed.

After my visit home, I resumed military duty, following orders to show up at Fort Ord, California. Once there, I was given a chance to make Sergeant again while training other recruits, but I couldn't handle it. Most of these kids were still tied to their mother's apron strings. How could I harden them so they could survive the cruel war? I didn't want any more boys to die in the war!

My drinking became worse. My anger and fighting were now part of a daily routine. While other soldiers talked about the war, blaming the Army for this or that, I would get confrontational. I was like a firecracker going off in all directions! I resented that a lot of these guys were career officers and never set foot on the battlefield. This fueled my anger further.

Proverbs 10:19 – Too much talk leads to sin. Be sensible and keep your mouth shut."

Nothing prepared me for the heartbreaking news of my favorite uncle passing away. I dropped everything and made my way back to Brooklyn so I could mourn my Uncle Mac. He had served in Europe during WWII, just five years before. He was the kindest, most genuine, caring person, always thinking about others, especially me. He was my hero.

I must have been like a tornado to my family and friends. I couldn't contain the anger, guilt, and bitterness. I lashed out with harsh words. The only thing putting me down were the severe headaches and seizures. I was still coughing up blood. I was also scratching my legs till they bled because I felt like bugs were crawling on me.

In our neighborhood there were many WWII vets. They knew me growing up. They kept begging me, "Go back to the base and get help."

During the day, I would pick up my clean, starched shirts from the local Chinese cleaners, but by nighttime, I looked like I had been in a war all over again. Stumbling back into our house after a rough night, I was met by my grandfather. Seeing tears on his face undid me and I finally agreed to return to Fort Dix, which was the closest base to home.

The return was at first uneventful except for feeling horribly sick. I couldn't explain my situation and found myself hauled off to a black box. Outside solitary confinement in a stockade was punishing in the dead of winter! I was deemed not having an excusable reason for being AWOL and was stripped down to nothing. For seven days I received only bread and water!

Psalm 88:4-8 "I am as good as dead, like a strong man with no strength left. They have left me among the dead, and I lie like a corpse in a grave.

I am forgotten, cut off from your care. You have thrown me into the lowest pit, into the darkest depths. Your anger weighs me down; with wave after wave you have engulfed me. You have driven my friends away by making me repulsive to them I am in a trap with no way of escape."

If I had anger issues before, now I was a raging animal! They wouldn't let me salute the flag, so I did it anyway! I did it in reverence of those who served and didn't make it home, and the many who were still fighting over there. I took a few beatings for this, but it didn't matter anymore.

I found myself bullied by officers. One sergeant flicked his smoking cigarette on the ground and asked me to pick it up. As I was bending over, he came up to me and kicked me hard in the groin. I was ready to attack and battle him. Quickly I was hauled away from behind and taken before the General's office. Amid the threats by those dragging me there, I actually became calmer. I realized this was my new battlefield. I was fighting a system that didn't allow a veteran to explain himself, and also a system that allowed bullies to physically hurt others. We were in a stockade that had housed WWII prisoners of war, mostly from Italy, and it seemed the camp personnel were still prejudiced against Italians!

I wasn't the only one to get picked on. Another disabled war veteran was thrown bodily against the wall of a urinal! To come to his defense, I got a couple of black and blues! This is around the time I met up with Quinn.

Psalm 64:1-3 "O God, listen to my complaint. Protect my life from my enemies ' threats. Hide me from the plots of this evil mob, from this gang of wrongdoers. The sharpen their tongues like swords and aim their bitter words like arrows."

The General, a very imposing figure, was sitting behind his desk. He clearly was not happy about wasting his time with a delinquent. Before asking me a single question, he threatened me.

"Your behavior is unacceptable for a soldier! I am going to send you to Korea!"

Laughing, I replied, "I've been there and back, sir!"

That caught him off guard. "Where were you stationed, Private?"

I started to tell him about the battles I had fought in. I couldn't remember places, but battle names I could never forget. That sparked his interest. He told me he had been in the May Massacre! I told him that was where I was shot after being knocked out by a concussion grenade. I had to confirm a few other details. He mellowed and at one point I thought he was going to come and hug me. He shouted back at the other officers, giving them orders.

"Get this man needed medical treatment, not the stockade! He was in Korea with me!"

Proverbs 10:8-9 "But correct the wise and they will love you. Instruct the wise and they will be even wiser."

Truce delegations

Truce delegations

Truce delegations

CHAPTER 16

Overwhelming Obstacles, Oppositions, and Ordeals

With long life I will satisfy him, And show him My salvation.
~ Psalm 91:16 (NKJV)

My father, who had been standing outside the stockade fence waiting to visit me, witnessed the entire scuffle between the officer and myself.

He was ready to climb the fence and come to my defense! He calmed down only when he saw me coming out of the General's office. I quickly told him the good news, that I would be receiving medical attention from the Army. I was taken to Walter Reed Army Hospital and also Valley Forge. My parents were relieved that I was receiving the best treatment possible and visited me often. I remember that it was my father who came more often. Mom chose to stay home to watch the grocery store.

After many consultations, most of the tests centered around my head injury. I went in for neurosurgery where the doctor said he would try to remove the shrapnel. I received local anesthesia for this procedure, but was made to stay awake while the doctor kept asking me questions. He told me it was the only way he would know if he was touching an important nerve in the brain. My skull being sawed apart felt like the buzzing of a dentist's drill in my head. There was no bullet. It had gone through the skull and arced within the helmet and came out making a second hole. This explains the sketch that Sergeant Nick, who found me, drew with two holes in the helmet. In the end, the final result was that they couldn't remove the shrapnel they did find. The doctor concluded it was too close to the brain, making it dangerous and further inoperable. They told me I had swelling in the brain.

(When Sal was shot in the head, he remembered a story of someone who had a bullet arc in his helmet and come out of the helmet making two holes side by side. This may have been what happened to Sal because no bullet had been removed according to his testimony or medical records. There was evidence of being shot through the skull, leaving shrapnel near his brain. When taken to Osaka Hospital in Japan, they only patched him up since it was very dangerous to operate in the head. When operated on in Valley Forge, the doctor told Sal the shrapnel was too close to the brain and therefore inoperable for removal, even though they sawed through his skull.)

According to medical records obtained later in life, I had a brain tumor! This probably accounted for my seizures and blackouts. Could this also contribute to the mood swings, anger, depression, and paranoia I was feeling?

I would have to wear a skullcap for quite some time. This made me look Jewish.

Back in New York, at the Veterans Administration, I would be questioned under sodium pentothal, an injected truth serum. Time and again I would be re-examined. I even underwent chemotherapy, thinking it was antibiotics for the chills and fevers. I was told I had black spots on my lungs. The lungs were so bad that I was questioned several times about getting tuberculosis while overseas. (From medical records obtained later in Florida, I read about receiving the chemotherapy.)

Born with brown eyes, my records and identifications had to be changed because now my eyes were circled blue. Doctors called this "arcus-senilis," an old-age symptom. I was only 20 years old!

My seizures continued. Science in the field of head trauma and post-traumatic stress disorders was still in its infancy. None of this made my nightmares go away! Not until the Vietnam War would soldiers come back and be diagnosed with traumas. Opioids were heavily prescribed.

I was hurt emotionally, relationally, physically, and spiritually! The extent of my wounds could not be seen. I could not reveal the extent of the battles inside me for fear of imprisonment in an asylum. This was the '50s way of dealing with extreme cases of anxiety. Electric shock treatments and getting hosed were corporal punishment for the ward. Not allowing this to continue, my family stepped in. They brought me back home.

Psalm 55:17-18 "Morning, noon, and night I cry out in my distress, and the Lord hears my voice. He ransoms me and keeps me safe from the battle waged against me."

An Army Board hearing was set to reevaluate my records. I needed the testimony of Sergeant Quinn, who was in the stockade with me. He also was in the same infantry company with me in Korea. My records were really messed up and at that time morning reports were not available to show the times I was wounded and returned to duty. A neighbor veteran and also my family doctor came to lend their support in helping me get a temporary disability from the Army to recover from the worst of the bodily traumas. Eventually I was retired from the military and moved to Florida where I raised my family.

Jeremiah 31:9 – "Tears of joy will stream down their faces, and I will lead them home with great care. They will walk beside quiet streams and on smooth paths where they will not stumble."

The situation might have seemed ideal, but in actuality, not having any support team and beginning anew led me to feel alone again to fight my demons. Who could understand the trauma of war, except fellow soldiers who shared that same trauma? I went to the Veterans Administration. However, it was now being overrun by Vietnam veterans. Those I encountered were having issues of drug abuse rather than the wounds from combat. The seriously wounded soldiers were being treated in major Army hospitals, not a small Army base. I couldn't understand the generational change that had veterans cursing their patriotism and our country's war haters cursing our veterans. I hated war too but one has to understand the need to defend one's beliefs and stand behind our country! I was seeing long-haired hippies smoking pot. They looked like they hadn't bathed in months. I did not go back to the VA for fear of my anger getting the best of me and starting fights.

In words offered to us by General Matthew Ridgway, Commander of the Eighth U.S. Army during the Korean War and which hold true for every generation in the future:

"We are here because of the decisions of the properly constituted authority of our respective governments. The loyalty we give and expect precludes any slightest questioning of these orders! What we fought for is not confined to Korea or our allies, but to our U.S. freedoms. The issues now joined right here in Korea are whether communism or individual freedoms shall prevail; whether the flight of fear driven people we have witnessed here shall be checked, or shall at some future time, however distant, engulf our own loved ones in all its misery and despair!"

These are the values my men and I fought for. We stood our ground at the 38th Parallel. We fought on freedom's side!

We judge when we feel judged; we hate when we hate ourselves! The need for self-worth led me to suffer emotional pain, resulting in much anger and hurt. It is simply natural after years of deflecting incessant bullying from peers, implying I was never good enough. At some critical stage, I retaliated and threw back accusations of my own!

I was keeping myself away from my miracle of healing. I started believing the opposite of God's Word. I had turned from Him and made my bed in a wretched, caged state of hell. But in His love, my actions had not stopped His love. When no one could fathom the depth of my suffering and afflictions, God came through!

1 John 3:1 "See how very much ourFather loves us, for he calls us his children, and that is what we are! But the people who belong to this world don't recognize that we are God's children because they don't know him.

How many times had I failed to see His miracles? How many times had I not seen His Glory revealed to me? All I saw instead was my mess and my less-than-perfect self.

Rather than striving to win acceptance of others, or value myself only when performing extreme actions, I should have looked to Our Heavenly Father who is the only one who has the right to define us!

Once when driving to Fort Hood, Texas, I witnessed a car accident where a car immediately burst into flames. Without hesitation I ran to the driver who was wedged in and pulled him from the burning vehicle. We were safely away when the car exploded. Once the emergency team arrived, I knew the driver would be taken care of. I left without further ado. I always felt compelled to do the daring, especially if it concerned saving someone. I realize now I was trying to redeem myself. How foolish! I was already redeemed by the Great I Am!

Isaiah 63:9 – "In all their suffering, he also suffered, and he personally rescued them. In his love and mercy he redeemed them. He lifted them up and carried them."

I couldn't find my way around the corner from home without getting lost, but thank God, my Savior was faithful, watching out for me!

Matthew 16:26 – "And what do you benefit if you gain the whole world but lose your own soul? Is anything worth more than your soul?"

Our feelings are like an idol, just as pride and envy are. If one lives by superiority, this is a lie and we are eventually led astray. I needed to be honest about my feelings, using them to determine how to respond to situations. Had I based my life on a lie or a truth? What does God's Word say?

2 Corinthians 10:12 – "Oh don't worry, we wouldn't dare say that we are as wonderful as these other men who tell you how important they are! But they are only comparing themselves with each other, using themselves as the standard of measurement. How ignorant!"

Just as we acknowledge how God sees others, we need to accept and embrace how He sees us! How He sees me! Godliness is wanting and seeking God to inspire us to be what we know we could be in Him.

1 John 4:16 – "We know how much God loves us and we have put our trust in his love. God is love, and all who live in love live in God, and God lives in them."

I would continue to experience monstrous migraines and many of the same symptoms I had after the war, but now it appeared I had to worry about a tumor growing from my lungs against my spine as I got older. It crippled me. In the hospital, the doctors held very little hope and asked the family to gather, since I was given just days to live. I remember looking to my wife for encouragement and found her praying. Her next words gave me hope: "There is no one but God who can tell you when it is your time. You do what you know to do to get better!"

Within moments, there was a commotion down the hall from my room in the hospital. Ladies from a Gospel church were making their way into my room. The leader of the group politely asked me if they could pray and sing, worshiping God with me. In my weakened condition, what I couldn't do for myself, I now had angels doing for me! Black angels who sang like a heavenly choir!

I knew I had to accept what my good doctors were doing, preparing me for my first treatment of radiation that evening. By the next morning, I got out of bed to use the restroom. One of my doctors came in just as I headed back to bed. The look of shock on his face was priceless! The tumor had shrunk and no longer pressed against my spine! I would continue to astonish the doctors by living many more years.

Psalm 30:1-3 "I will exalt you, Lord, for you rescued me. You refused to let my enemies triumph over me. O Lord my God, I cried to you for help, and you restored my health. You brought me up from the grave, O Lord. You kept me from falling into the pit of death."

It became important for me to measure up to the goals the Lord gave me. I know I will be judged by Jesus when I stand before Him! I am grateful for being able to share about the Korean War, and to remember those who served alongside me in the Army of the United States of America. Grateful for the opportunity to be a dutiful son to God and for my country. I will try my best.

God kept His promises. He had mercy on my soul! My long life and last days were most peaceful. The Veterans Administration did all they could for me so that I remained at home, receiving care and medicines as needed.

I had an Army nurse who came by my bedside, helping me with patience and kindness. She quickly put me at ease. On my last night on earth, she arrived even though she wasn't on call. She had a dream the evening before about her father. He told her, "Take care of my buddy Sal!" No one else knew that was the way I signed my photos that I gave out to those I knew and served alongside. During the long vigil, as she spoke with my wife, we learned that her father was in Korea with me. He was one of the tankers who paved the way so soldiers could follow and they were the same battles I was in.

Their spirits come to guide me home. The pain is gone. I now rest in peace.

Jeremiah 31:9 – "Tears of joy will stream down their faces, and I will lead them home with great care."

Portrait of Sal drawn by Sgt. Nick

The United States of America
honors the memory of
Salvatore Vincent Macaluso
This certificate is awarded by a grateful
nation in recognition of devoted and
selfless consecration to the service
of our country in the Armed Forces
of the United States.

President of the United States

Certificate of a Grateful Nation by President to Sal

United States
Second Infantry Division
Korea 1950-51

CERTIFICATE OF COMMENDATION

As First Sergeant of Company "C", 38th Infantry Regiment, Second U.S. Infantry Division, I hereby commend highly

PFC SALVATORE V. MACALUSO

For his devotion to duty, courage and indomitable fighting spirit displayed as a Combat Infantryman in the service of his country against the armed enemy forces of Communist North Korea and the Chinese volunteers while assigned to "Charging Charlie" Company.

Therefore, by having distinguished yourself in such combat engagements as The Battle of Wonju - Chipyong Ni, Operation Killer and Ripper, The Chinese Spring Offensive, Fool Mountain, Bloody Ridge, Heartbreak Ridge, as well as other hostile campaigns against a numerically superior enemy force, you shall long be remembered by both your comrades-in-arms and a grateful nation.

The Esprit De Corps and loyalty demonstrated by you to both your comrades and your unit while under the most adverse and difficult conditions of the time are in keeping with the highest standards and traditions of the United States Army.

Your bravery, competence and outstanding achievements as a combat warrior have contributed greatly in helping maintain the Second Division's most honored and prestigious motto of "Second To None."

In grateful recognition,

Lynn L. Nichols, M/Sgt., RA12&&2690
Company "C", 38th Infantry Regiment
2nd Division

Certificate of Commendation from Sgt. Nick to Sal

June 25, 2000

Dear Veteran

On the occasion of the 50th anniversary of the outbreak of the Korean War, I would like to offer you my deepest gratitude for your noble contribution to the efforts to safeguard the Republic of Korea and uphold liberal democracy around the world. At the same time, I remember with endless respect and affection those who sacrificed their lives for that cause.

We Koreans hold dear in our hearts the conviction, courage and spirit of sacrifice shown to us by such selfless friends as you, who enabled us to remain a free democratic nation.

The ideals of democracy, for which you were willing to sacrifice your all 50 years ago, have become universal values in this new century :ium.

a century after the Korean War, we honor you and reaffirm which helped to forge the blood alliance between our two .s. Anu resolve once again to work with all friendly nations good of humankind and peace in the world.

ank you once again for your noble sacrifice, and pray for your niness.

Sincerely yours,

signed

Kim Dae-jung
nt of R blic of Korea

감사 서한
Letter of Appreciation

Letter of Appreciation from Rep. of Korea in English

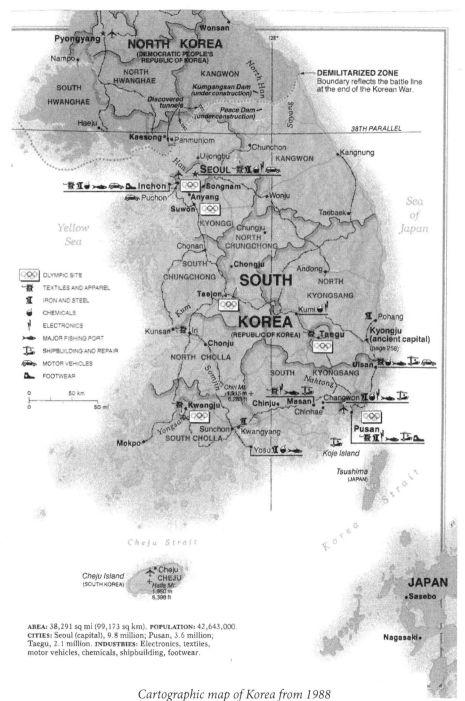

AREA: 38,291 sq mi (99,173 sq km). **POPULATION:** 42,643,000.
CITIES: Seoul (capital), 9.8 million; Pusan, 3.6 million;
Taegu, 2.1 million. **INDUSTRIES:** Electronics, textiles,
motor vehicles, chemicals, shipbuilding, footwear.

Cartographic map of Korea from 1988

Docks and fleets of South Korea

Village elder and children by storefront

CONCLUSION

To you heroes who proved that armor is iron but man is steel against an army whose guns rattled at dawn, I look back and see your faces. Brokenhearted, I fervently pray that there be no more wars, but a time of peace. Remember God's promises.

Jeremiah 1: 17-18 "Therefore you, gird up your loins! .... Do not be dismayed and break down at the sight of their faces.... For l, behold I have made you this day a fortified city and an iron pillar and brazen walls against the whole land.... {giving you divine strength which no hostile power can overcome}."

Jeremiah 6:27 "l (says the Lord) have set you as an assayer and a prover of ore among My people, that you may know and try their doings and be like a watchtower."

Jeremiah 15:20 "And I will make you to this people a fortified, bronze wall; they will fight against you, but they will not prevail over you, for I am with you to save and deliver you, says the Lord."

Jeremiah 29:11 "For I know the thoughts and plans that I have for you, says the LORD, thoughts and plans for welfare and peace and not for evil, to give you hope in your final outcome."

lsaiah 41:10 "Fear not, for I am with you; do not look around you in terror and be dismayed, for I am your God. I will strengthen and harden you to difficulties, yes, I will help you; yes, I will hold you up and retain you with My right hand of rightness and justice."

lsaiah 49:10 "Behold I have refined you...."

Isaiah 50:7 "For the Lord God helps me; therefore, have I not been ashamed or confounded. Therefore, have I set my face like a flint, and I know that I shall not be put to shame."

Joshua 1:5-7,9 "No man shall be able to stand before you all the days of your life. As I was with Moses, so I will be with you; I will not fail you or forsake you. Be strong and of good courage, for you shall cause this people to inherit the land which I swore to their fathers to give them. Only you be strong and very courageous, that you may do according to all the law.... Have I not commanded you? Be strong, vigorous, and very courageous. Be not afraid, neither be dismayed, for the Lord your God is with you wherever you go."

Hebrew 13:5 "..... for He Himself has said, I will not in any way fail you nor give you up nor leave you without support. I will not, I will not, I will not in any degree leave you helpless nor forsake, nor let you down. Assuredly not!"

2 Timothy 1:7 "For God did not give us a spirit of timidity, but He has given us a spirit of power and of love and of calm and well-balanced mind and discipline and self-control."

2 Corinthians 13:10-14 "So I write these things........ for building you up and not for tearing you down.

Finally, brethren, farewell! Be strengthened; be encouraged and consoled and comforted; be of the same mind one another; live in peace and the God of love and the Author and Promoter of peace will be with you. Greet one another with a consecrated kiss. All the people of God here salute you. The grace of the Lord Jesus Christ and the love of God and the presence and fellowship in the Holy Spirit be with you all. AMEN"

REFERENCES

AARP magazine, edition July/August 2003 (pages 51-52)

Bible Scriptures quoted from the New King James Version, and the New Living Translation Version

DAV magazine, edition January/February 2000 (page 25)

Escape and Evasion by Charles Winder

Korean War Branch Casualty List, for 1950 – 1953

National Geographic magazine, August 1988

Reader's Digest magazine, December 1951 (pages 45-48)

Second to None: The Second United States Infantry Division in Korea, 1950 – 1951, Lt. Clark Monroe

Smithsonian magazine, July 2003

The American Legion magazine, July 1993

The Bloody Road to Panmunjom by Edwin P. Hoyt

The Forgotten War: America in Korea, 1950-1953 by Clay Blair

The River and the Gauntlet by S.L.A. Marshall

The Running Wounded: A Personal Memory of the Korean War by William W. Day IV

America's Tenth Legion: The X Corps in Korea, 1950 by Shelby L. Stanton

This is War! Photo-Narrative of the Korean War by David Douglas Duncan

This Kind of War by T. R. Fehrenbach

VFW Memorial Edition, 1954, *Pictorial History of Korean War*

VFW Magazines, editions - June/1988; June/July 1990; December/1991; June/July 1993; October, November and December/2000; January, February, March, April and May/2001; August, September/2001; January 2002; June/July 2002; February 2003; and September 2003.